soulsister

connect
The Lowdown on Friendships and Relationships

Kendall Payne

Regal

From Gospel Light
Ventura, California, U.S.A.

Gospel Light is a Christian publisher dedicated to serving the local church. We believe God's vision for Gospel Light is to provide church leaders with biblical, user-friendly materials that will help them evangelize, disciple and minister to children, youth and families.

It is our prayer that this Gospel Light resource will help you discover biblical truth for your own life and help you minister to youth. May God richly bless you.

For a free catalog of resources from Gospel Light, please contact your Christian supplier or contact us at 1-800-4-GOSPEL or www.gospellight.com.

PUBLISHING STAFF

William T. Greig, Publisher • **Dr. Elmer L. Towns,** Senior Consulting Publisher • **Alex Field,** Acquisition Editor • **Jessie Minassian,** Assistant Editor • **Bayard Taylor,** M.Div., Senior Editor, Biblical and Theological Issues

ISBN 0-8307-3731-6
© 2005 Gospel Light
All rights reserved.
Printed in the U.S.A.

table of contents

part one:
boy meets girl

one: failure
The Only Option

Neither he who plants nor he who waters is anything,
but only God, who makes things grow.
1 Corinthians 3:7

He who began a good work in you will carry it on
to completion until the day of Jesus Christ.
Philippians 1:6

I am very excited that you have chosen to pick this book up and read it. I hope it challenges you. If you are changed at all in the next 12 chapters, I cannot take credit for it, but that's just fine with me! Like 1 Corinthians 3:7 says, one man plants the seed and another waters it—but *only* God makes things grow.

Let me say right off the bat (so there is no confusion) that this workbook is intended to be very interactive. In other words, you have to *participate* in order to get the most out of it. You can't just passively read along and expect it to soak into your brain through your eyeballs. You have to invest yourself in it.

So go find your favorite pen (if you have one) and get your mind in gear. Wherever you see 💬, I am expecting you to talk to me! These sections are all about you—what you think and feel, what you're processing, what you're questioning, what you wholeheartedly believe—*anything* goes. And I would love for you to start a journal totally separate from this workbook if you find you have more to say.

Okay, here's a journal section for practice.

💬 **What experiences have you had with Christian books in the past? Do you dig them? Are you worried that this one's going to be lame? (Go ahead—be honest. I don't have subversive spies on the lookout.)**

Are you the kind of person who consistently reads a chapter a day? Or do you forget you're even reading a book, find it a month later, and then read half of it in one sitting?

I remember reading Christian workbooks and thinking they were so lame. They pretended to relate, but never really did. They were full of cheesy curriculum and even cheesier questions. So know that I'm committed to making this workbook relevant to your life. I'm going to tell it like it is, no matter how painful that may be for my ego. And if you get to the end and think, *That was lame*, at least it will make a very artsy coaster.

One other disclaimer before we get started: Throughout the book you will read honest accounts of my dating and life experiences, and you may find that you disagree with my commentary or philosophy. Great! Please know that you *do not* have to agree with everything I say; I'm human too, trying to figure out this life just as you are! If you're not sure about something I've said, take it to your journal. That's how you develop your own opinions. Never accept anyone's advice without first testing it (1) against Scripture (which will force you to read your Bible), (2) in your own heart (does it resonate with your spirit?) and (3) with wise counsel (like your parents, your youth pastor or a "big sis"). Most important, allow God to grow you through the process.

Alrighty then—Let's get started!

Falling Short

For all have sinned and fall short of the glory of God.
Romans 3:23

The media loves to tell the dramatic story of a person's rise to fame and all the painful rejections that they endured to get there—but only once they're famous. Until then no one cares. Only when we reach the prize do we then look back over the pitted landscape and say unashamedly, "All of those experiences have made me who I am." Take Albert Einstein for example. He took an entrance exam for the Swiss Federal Institute of Technology—and *failed!* (In case that name doesn't ring a bell, he later went on to become one of the greatest mathematical minds of our century.)

Since most of us haven't achieved genius, movie star or millionaire status, failure still isn't vogue for us; and so our hearts become convinced that to stumble or slip up is not acceptable in this world. Our families, our schools, our workplaces, even our own personalities—we're being told from all angles that "failure is not an option."

But I believe failure is the *only* option.

> Can you think of any other historical or modern-day heroes who had failed attempts but never gave up? How does that inspire you in your own quest for success?

Romans 3:23 tells us that we aren't perfect. We've all set out at some point to accomplish something, only to be met with devastating disappointment. Our pride then gets pummeled against the rocks of our own inabilities. We are unable to pull ourselves up by our bootstraps when we need to the most. Paul writes candidly about his own experience with these feelings.

To keep me from becoming conceited . . . there was given me a thorn in my flesh. Three times I pleaded with the Lord to take it away from me. But he said to me, "My grace is sufficient for you, for my power is made perfect in weakness." Therefore I will boast all the more gladly about my weaknesses, so that Christ's power may rest on me. That is why, for Christ's sake, I delight in weaknesses. . . . For when I am weak, then I am strong.
2 Corinthians 12:7-10

The sooner we accept our failures, the more successful we can potentially become. Our failures expose our weaknesses and reveal our desperate need for God. Now what we do with that failure is the real question. Do we turn *to* God or *from* God in those moments?

💬 **Are you afraid of failure, or do you accept it as a part of life? Are you aware of your own failures, or do you think you've got it all under control? How do you think God views your failures?**

💬 **Make a list of three things you view as failures in your life.**

1.

2.

3.

💬 **Now use your imagination and try to turn each failure into a possible strength. How can God use these failures to teach you, grow you and make you stronger? (If you feel deep shame concerning these failures and can't imagine how God could ever use them, ask Him right now to help you see how He can use them for good.)**

We will only learn that God's grace is sufficient when we become painfully aware of our shortcomings. If we live our entire lives void of disappointment (which is the goal of most people's existence), we will never cling to Christ. Instead, we will continue to believe that *we* have the power to do anything and everything right on our own.

Embracing the Challenge

So we are transfigured much like the Messiah, our lives gradually becoming brighter and more beautiful as God enters our lives and we become like him.
2 Corinthians 3:18, *The Message*

So what does all this have to do with relationships? Glad you asked.

Contrary to Hollywood fairy tales, the truth is that if you choose to make yourself vulnerable by entering into a relationship with a member of the opposite sex, you *will* experience hurt. You may even experience failure. I know I have. That's why I want to challenge you to embrace your weakness right now, not in retrospect. Embracing our own weakness is one of the ways God chooses to teach us and draw us back to Himself.

A *fear* of failure will never make a person successful; it will only paralyze his or her potential. I have had failure after failure (after *failure*), but each one has been a part of my success, and I would not trade them for gold, silver or diamonds (and I love diamonds!).

I only hope that through reading about *my* mistakes you won't make the same blunders in your own life. I hope that you will become a little more mature as you read about my immaturity. I hope that you will become a little wiser as you read about my foolish escapades. And I hope that you might have success because of reading about my failures.

I am looking forward to a lifetime of errors,

💬 If you were to write a book about your dating relationships, would you be proud of how you've handled yourself or would you have to omit certain chapters? What subjects would you rather not talk about?

💬 If you haven't entered into the realm of dating relationships (which I totally support and respect), what failures do you already know you want to avoid because of watching others' mistakes or from hearing wise advice?

shortcomings and the exposure of everything I try to hide from, because—here's the key—I know that God is faithful to teach me through them in order that I might become more like Him. I know your relationships will not be devoid of devastating failures either; I only hope that you learn from them, grow from them and see God in a brand-new way.

My mother has a slip of paper hanging on her bulletin board that says, "The definition of insanity is doing the same thing over and over again but expecting a different result." Nothing could be closer to the truth in my own life! I have gotten into relationship after relationship assuming that because the boy had changed, so had I. This led me down a path of volatile, dysfunctional romances that all ended the exact same way: broken. But I rejoice that each one has taught me something new, although at the time, it was quite painful to learn. You might know the saying, "Hindsight is 20/20"; well, I believe it!

In your dating relationships you will also likely face many trying situations. You will have to decide what you want in life. Some decisions will be easy; others will be painful. I pray that you will hold on during the difficult times. And I hope that you will begin to view them as gifts from God.

JOIN ME IN THIS PRAYER:

Father God,

I thank You for giving me life—not a monotonous, boring existence, but a life that is full of adventure. Give me an outlook and attitude that embraces all experiences—even the painful ones. Give me the strength to endure when times are tough. Give me comfort when I cannot carry on. Give me grace, that I might extend it to others and also to myself. More than anything else, just give me You, and that will be enough! So be it.

{ At my home church instead of ending a prayer with "amen" we say, "So be it," because that's what amen really means. }

the two: nonquestion

Before we get started answering the nonquestion (is that possible?), I want you to take a few moments to write down your thoughts about the idea of dating (or "going out," or whatever you and your friends call having a romantic relationship with a guy). Take some time to think about each topic before you answer. Remember that some of your answers will depend on your age, your experiences and your parents' wishes, so your answers may change as time passes.

- **When do you think a girl is old enough to start dating? Do you think there's one age, or is it different for every girl?**

- **What guidelines (aka rules) have your parents given you concerning dating? Have they given you permission to date at a certain age, in groups only, etc.?**

- **Do you require any nonnegotiable characteristics when choosing someone to date? (For example, "He has to be a Christian," "He has to respect my desire to save sex for marriage," "He has to share my passion for laser tag," etc.)**

💬 How would you like your dating life to go? Do you want your first love to be your last love? Do you want to date different guys, like tasting samples at Costco? Do you want to stay "just friends" with guys until a certain time in life?

💬 Do you think God has an opinion about dating? What do you suppose He thinks?

You can (and should) begin forming ideas, standards and boundaries about dating, even if you're not dating anyone at this moment. For some reason, we have a much harder time trying to formulate those things when we're starry-eyed in love (or even "like"). So it's a good idea to decide what we will and won't do, and who we will and won't date, before we get into a relationship.

Realizing Your Passions

I think I qualify as a first-rate *Lord of the Rings* freak. I love the imagery, the story, the lessons and the characters. I had no clue the books even existed before the movies came out, but I've definitely made up for lost time. I saw *The Fellowship of the Ring* in London, England, on a cold December day. When I emerged from the theater, the intensity of Frodo's quest was so real to me, and I identified so deeply with his character, I could have sworn the Orcs were hunting me too! I sprinted to the train, afraid that if I slowed down, they'd catch me and make me tell them where the ring was.

Now, I'm a songwriter at heart, and I love to craft the perfect analogies for my feelings. But for about two or three years, every analogy became something involving *The Lord of the Rings*. I found myself saying, "That reminds me of when Aragorn said 'The same blood runs in my veins . . . the same weakness!'" or, "I feel just like Bilbo when he says, 'Stretched . . . like butter over too much bread.'"

One day I was at a church service and the pastor used clips from *The Lord of the Rings* to illustrate his point. I hadn't seen the movies in a month or two, and when Gandolf, Legolas and Sam came on the screen, I felt like they were my long-lost brothers. I wanted to hug them. I wanted to sit down over a nice cup of coffee and catch up on life. This is how freakish I had become!

● Do you have any strange and harmless obsessions? Write down some of your favorite pastimes. (All of a sudden I hear Julie Andrews singing the words "Raindrops on Roses" from *The Sound of Music*—scary!)

● What are you passionate about? Patriotism? College? Work? Travel? The great outdoors? Music? Medicine? What lights your fire? Why do you get up every morning? (And I don't mean because your alarm goes off, or because your mom threatens your life if you don't.)

making Passionate Choices

Greater love has no one than this, that he lay down his life for his friends.
John 15:13

Do not be yoked together with unbelievers. For what do righteousness and wickedness have in common? Or what fellowship can light have with darkness? . . .
What does a believer have in common with an unbeliever? What agreement is there between the temple of God and idols?
2 Corinthians 6:14-16

I have a friend who is a fireman. His grandfather was a fireman, his father was a fireman, and from the time he was a small boy, he dreamt of becoming one himself. This year he has finally gotten a position with the fire department. He takes his job very seriously, and he must keep extremely physically fit. On Thanksgiving, when most Americans take the day off to relax, eat until they can't see straight and then pass out on the couch only to wake up with a trypto-phan hangover, my friend the fireman set his alarm for 6 a.m. First, he went surfing. After lunch, he went mountain biking. He makes me feel so lazy! He also goes to bed at 9 p.m. to make sure he has the energy for whatever may come the next day. Now that you're feeling guilty too, I'll get to the point: Like it or not, our passions dictate our choices. That's how we measure our love for something—we only truly love the things for which we are willing to sacrifice.

Jesus showed His passionate love for humanity when He willingly went to the cross. He said, "No more talking about how much I love you; let Me show you." He bled and He died because passion is more than words; it requires action.

Whether you know it or not, you will place the things you are most passionate about at the top of your priorities list. Everything else will trail behind. If your number one passion is Christ, naturally you will make choices that reflect that passion. So that brings us to "the question": Can (or should) someone whose number one passion is Christ fall in love with someone who doesn't share that passion? If your answer is yes, I can offer only this conclusion: You must not be as passionate as you say you are.

💬 How does that next-to-the-last sentence make you feel? Are you offended? Can you see why I would come to that conclusion? If you disagree, explain why.

I've had more than one young woman tell me her story about meeting a boy who is everything she could ever want—except a Christian. My response to her is always, "Then he's obviously not everything you've ever wanted— quit lying to yourself." It might sound mean, it might sound harsh, but sometimes the truth just plain hurts.

💬 When Christ let His passion dictate His actions (by dying on the cross), you were the benefactor. How do you think He feels when you say that you're passionate about Him, but you don't show it in the things you do or the guys you date?

Discovering the Roots
of Your Passion

My dad used to make me pull weeds on hot summer days. I hated it. He seemed to think there was some value in getting sweaty and sore, but he had trouble instilling that value in his two Malibu-native daughters. We would avoid it for so long that the tangle of weeds always seemed insurmountable.

One day I made the mistake of asking my father why we couldn't just mow the whole thing down. He took me outside and squatted down beside a massive weed and gripped it with his right hand. With all his might he pulled. He braced his left hand over his right and pulled again. He leaned back at a 90-degree angle and used all his body weight to unearth the pesky bugger. Finally, it gave up the fight and came out of the ground. When my dad regained his balance, he turned the leafy weed upside down and stuck the dirty side in my face. He said, "Do you know what these are? Roots. And if you don't get to the root of the problem, you're just wasting your time."

💬 **What are the roots below the surface that keep you from giving your whole heart to Jesus? This is going to require you to be very honest with yourself. If you're not up for the challenge, it's okay to leave this section blank. But please, please, please don't come up with some fake, cheesy answer.**

Now I want you to imagine that you and I are best friends. I own a wonderful house (I love imagination!), and you always come to visit me. Sometimes you stop by for coffee before school in the mornings, and most nights we cook dinner for each other and talk for hours. Some weekends we laugh till the sun comes up; other nights are filled with sweet tears. And when we aren't under the same roof, we talk on the phone and text message each other incessantly. We have so much fun when we are together.

One day you find a new friend. I'm overjoyed at first. Any friend of yours is a friend of mine! The more the merrier, I always say!

But this new friend doesn't want to meet me. This new friend doesn't want to spend his evenings hanging out at my house. This new friend takes you away from me. And I can't help but be sad—but I let you go. I would never force you to spend time with me. If you'd rather be with that friend than with me, then I want you to be happy. But please know that if you ever want to swing by and visit, even just for an hour or two, my door is always open.

You've probably already guessed where I'm going with this: You have to ask yourself, Do you really want to date a guy who will take you away from God? Or do you want to date a guy who goes to God with you? I'll be honest, when I think of "rules" and "musts" I want to rebel. If I'm not allowed to date a non-Christian, it only makes me want to do it more. But in my more mature moments, I realize that I'd be foolish to jeopardize my dreams in Christ just to be stubborn.

💬 **If you were the friend who was left behind, how would you feel? Angry? Jealous? Disappointed?**

💬 **Remember that I said it's important to decide what you will and won't do, and who you will and won't date, before you get into a relationship? Why might that especially apply to deciding whether you will date a non-Christian?**

Reserving Our Passion for Him

I speak the truth in Christ—I am not lying, my conscience confirms it in the Holy Spirit.

Romans 9:1

God wants us to speak truthfully. He loves when we look inside our hearts and are honest about what we find there. With that in mind, choose which of the following statements best describes you and circle it:

1. I like God. I *really* like God. But I do not *love* Him, because if I did I would be forced by my own passion to rearrange my lifestyle. And you know what, Kendall? I'm just not willing to do that. And so I'm going to date whomever *I* want because I don't care enough about my friendship with God. I only want to know what He thinks when it jives with what *I* think. I'm just not prepared to alter my decisions for Him.

2. I love God with all of my soul—more than anything in this world. And I am willing to back up my words with actions. When I look at my life, I see that I'm not perfect; there's still a tremendous amount of work to be done. But God has access to every area of my life, and when He asks something of me, I willingly surrender it (even if it takes me a day or two). I only want to be in a relationship with a guy who has this same passion for God.

Whichever statement you circled, know that God isn't done with you yet. My prayer is that you would begin to let God lavish you with the blessings that come only when we reserve our strongest passions for Him and *show it* by the way we live. Let's pray.

Lord,
help me see what is in my heart. I want to stand before You one day in full acknowledgment of my motives. Where I lack passion for You, please awaken it within me. And help me when I cannot help myself. So be it.

three:
KAH-MUE-NAH-KAY-SHUN

Do not be quick with your mouth, do not be hasty in your heart to utter anything before God.
God is in heaven and you are on earth, so let your words be few.

Ecclesiastes 5:2

Can you say "kah-mue-nah-kay-shun"? Sound it out . . . that's right! Let's explore the different ways that we communicate— with and without words. Chances are you're saying more than you realize without even opening your mouth.

The Bible tells us to let our words be few. God gave us two ears and one mouth— maybe it's time we get the hint! Only a small percentage of our communication is actually verbal.

💬 **What do you think Solomon (the writer of Ecclesiastes) meant when he said, "Let your words be few"? Did he mean it literally or figuratively? What kinds of words do you think he was referring to?**

the Power of Body Language

One day I was sitting at a coffee shop, fully engrossed in my laptop, my iTunes pumping over the headphones. I was typing away when two people caught my attention. They were sitting outside on a park bench. She was slender and blonde, he was tall and handsome; but I was not distracted by their physical appearance. I saw him wipe his face and I realized he was crying. I don't know why that interested me (okay, maybe I'm just nosey!), but I continued to watch out of the corner of my eye. (I thought I was so sneaky, but I'm sure I was totally obvious to everyone else in the coffee shop.)

What struck me as so odd was their body language. I couldn't hear a word these people were saying to each other, but it was as if their dialogue was being blasted through my headphones.

He was sitting on the left end of the bench, smashed up against the armrest, as if she had some infectious disease and he was desperate to not let her breathe on him. She sat a comfortable distance from him but close enough to show that they were more than just friends. She had her arm resting on the back of the bench, her entire torso twisted to face him. He, on the other hand, in between wiping the tears from his face, stared off to his right—the same direction his entire body was facing. She would touch him lovingly and he would respond with a cold shrug. It went on for an hour or so. Whatever they were talking about, it was highly distressing to him and not very upsetting to her—that I know for sure.

💬 What nonverbal ways do you communicate with people in general? When you're mad, do you pout, slouch or throw your shoulders back in defiance? How do you communicate when you're happy, confident or giddy?

💬 If you have a boyfriend now, how do you use body language to communicate with him when you're happy, angry or displeased? Do you get the desired response out of him when you act that way?

The Power of a Glance

When I was 19 years old, I lived with a friend in Beverly Hills, California. She had just graduated college and was living in a guesthouse. Now, when I say *house*, I don't mean a spare room. I mean a real, honest-to-goodness, three-bedroom, two-bathroom house. It was directly adjacent to her mom and dad's *mansion*. Anyway, back to my point. When my friend offered to let me rent a room at her place, I jumped at the opportunity.

We had so much fun living together; she was hysterically funny, and we spent many nights laughing until the sun came up. I had just ended a pretty intense relationship and my heart was recuperating, so during that season in my life I wasn't really interested in guys. She, on the other hand, had dates lined up for weeks. The phone was ringing off the hook. It seemed that every time she left the house she met someone who asked her out. So one day I asked her about it. Her response was something like this, "I don't know . . . I guess it's that extra couple seconds, ya know?"

I didn't know, and so I asked her to clarify. She said, "You know the moment when two people's eyes meet from across the room? You see someone and then immediately look away out of embarrassment?" Yeah, I knew all about that. It took me about two seconds to determine that I was attracted, after which time I'd immediately look away and try to seem really preoccupied. That's how I had always done it, and I assumed that's how *all* girls did it. But my friend continued, "Well, rather than look away, I just keep looking. Rather than look away after two or three seconds, wait till about five or six seconds before you look away. But don't just stare at him like a stalker—look friendly . . . smile or something."

It was a shocking revelation, one that I've been thankful for ever since. It's okay to be confident in who you are. Of course, the goal is not to play games or be an obnoxious flirt. The goal is to be yourself and to be *approachable* (i.e., a little less intimidating). You are one beautiful woman, and that is totally intimidating to a guy.

I gave my friend's advice a try, and I promise you it worked! Eye contact and big smiles— they work every time. In fact, they work so well, I need to offer a word of caution: Reserve this technique for guys that would actually be worth getting to know! The five-second rule is for guys at your church, youth group or other meeting ground for solid Christian young people. You don't want to be approachable to *all* men!

💬 **Are you shy or outgoing? Can you approach someone you've never met and talk about whatever comes to your mind? Or do you need to know someone before you'd ever consider striking up a conversation?**

THE POWER OF
CLOTHING

So let's review. The first way we communicate with members of the opposite gender is through body language: how we literally posture ourselves in someone's presence. We also communicate through what we wear on our bodies. The clothes we put on speak volumes about how we want to be looked at and treated.

I was recently sitting in a fast-food Mexican restaurant, eating a bean burrito, without a care in the world. A woman walked in. My back was to the door, but I knew it was a woman before I ever laid eyes on her. Every man in the restaurant looked up from his plate of nachos; even the kitchen staff whistled at each other and nodded in her direction. I knew she must have been wearing something revealing and, boy, was I right! She had some serious cleavage going on, and her blue jeans were so tight I was afraid they were cutting off her circulation. She sauntered in like she owned the place, and I watched every guy's head turn as if she were giving away free quesadillas.

Now every once in a while I get a very indignant, rambunctious streak that comes shivering up my spine, and this was one of those times. I had half a mind to get up, walk over to her and say in a very loud and condescending voice, "Do you know your boobies are about to fall out of your blouse?" But I restrained myself.

Part of me felt bad for her. I wondered if she realized that she looked like meat in a meat market. I wondered if she knew that as long as she dressed like that, no guy would respect her the way a man should respect a woman. I wondered what made her so desperate for attention that she would flaunt her body like it was all she had.

I love to look cute and wear clothes that are fashionable and flattering. That's not a bad thing! But when girls purposely wear low-cut tops, extra-short skirts or skin-tight pants just to get some heads to turn, they're using their sexuality as a tool to manipulate men. I hate to tell you, but if you look sexy in an outfit, most of the time you're only going to have middle-aged men staring at you—and that's just gross!

The wisest man who ever lived, King Solomon, had some good advice for young men. But I think this passage is good for us girls to hear too.

💬 When you get dressed, do you choose things that you know will draw attention to your body? Do you hope guys will notice you because of what you wear? Or do you choose to wear outfits based on how well they fit and how functional they are?

💬 If your clothes came equipped with a voice-message system, what would they declare to the people who see you throughout the day?

A. Too hot for you!
B. Sassy but sincere
C. Cute and friendly

My son, pay attention to my wisdom, listen well to my words of insight, that you may maintain discretion and your lips may preserve knowledge. For the lips of an adulteress drip honey, and her speech is smoother than oil; but in the end she is bitter as gall, sharp as a double-edged sword. Her feet go down to death; her steps lead straight to the grave. She gives no thought to the way of life; her paths are crooked, but she knows it not. Now then, my sons, listen to me; do not turn aside from what I say. Keep to a path far from her, do not go near the door of her house. May your fountain be blessed, and may you rejoice in the wife of your youth. A loving doe, a graceful deer—may her breasts satisfy you always, may you ever be captivated by her love. Why be captivated, my son, by an adulteress? Why embrace the bosom of another man's wife? For a man's ways are in full view of the Lord, and he examines all his paths. The evil deeds of a wicked man ensnare him; the cords of his sin hold him fast. He will die for lack of discipline, led astray by his own great folly.

Proverbs 5:1-8,18-23

💬 **What do you think this Scripture has to say to you? What sticks out? Which character do you identify with more: the dangerous woman or the wife of his youth?**

The Gift of Relationships

When you don't have something, you begin to think that you need it more than you actually do. If you really needed a man to survive, you'd be dead by now without one. If you don't have one now, then you can go on living. If you were to spend the rest of your life single, when you are on your deathbed your doctor would not say, "This woman is dying for lack of a significant relationship in her life." I hope that's obvious.

For some reason, we think that when we fall in love we will never be lonely again. Love makes such fools of smart people! There will always be pain in the journey, but also tremendous joy. And before God blesses us with someone we can fall head over heels for, and who will fall just as hard for us, we must develop the art of meaning what we say and saying what we mean—aka communication. It's one of the greatest gifts we can give someone we care so deeply about.

Father God,

open my eyes to my insecurities and shortcomings. Help me to see where I feel inadequate, and help me not to look to my human relationships to fill that void. Help me to come and lay it at Your feet instead. Teach me how to understand my emotions and communicate them in healthy ways, verbally and nonverbally.

So be it.

sayonara, four: sweetheart

We don't want to do it. The thought of it makes our stomachs turn and our blood go cold, but sometimes it must be done. Even worse, sometimes it *must* be done to us!

Breaking up is never easy. Nothing anyone can say will make the pain go away. But hopefully it won't all be in vain. Here's the secret: If you're committed to *learning* from the heartache, then the tiniest glimmer of hope will start to shine in you. You will begin to endure your sadness with a bit of patience and grace. Never underestimate hope; it's a powerful substance. Just give it time and it will grow.

suspicion Versus Selection

Above all else, guard your heart, for it is the wellspring of life.
Proverbs 4:23

God didn't make us with hearts of steel; we aren't invincible. That's why in Proverbs we are told to "guard" our hearts. They need protection. When I was younger, this Scripture conjured up images of some back alley in New York City. I'd envision myself clutching my purse tight to my body, wary of every doorway, giving the evil eye to every suspicious character that crossed my path.

Now when I read it, I think of myself as the sole guardian of a rare, endangered hot springs on a majestic, snow-covered mountain. People travel from all over the world to visit and behold its splendor, to sit in the steamy water and relish one of nature's greatest phenomenons. It just so happens that I am the only one who knows the trail that leads to the spring. I am also the only one who holds the key to unlock the gate. And so I sit at the bottom of the mountain, able to choose who gets to make the journey to the spring alongside me.

Do you see the difference in the two mentalities? One is *suspicious* and one is *selective*.

💬 **Think of a personal analogy for guarding your heart. Write it or draw it in this journal space.**

TIME TO GO

There are many good reasons to break up with someone—so many, in fact, that there's no way we could touch on each one here. So I'd like to share one of my experiences.

In one of my relationships, there came a point when my boyfriend shared some of the deepest secrets a man can hold in his heart. (On a side note, I highly encourage this sharing of dark, unspoken places many, *many* moons before the marriage question is even considered.) Out of respect for him, I will not divulge the information, but I would like to make you, the reader, aware of the enormity of his disclosure. Everyone is ashamed of or embarrassed to share something, but some of us have secrets that are so dark and dirty that they rarely, if ever, see the light of day.

I am grateful, even now, that he shared his struggles with me. I am still torn about how I responded to it. When I became aware of his painful past, I lost all ability to choose for myself what I desired in a mate. I decided that I would stick with him. I didn't want to, but I thought I had to.

💬 **Have you ever had to break up with someone? What did it take to get you to that point?**

💬 **Do you think there are "deal breakers" in relationships—those lines that, if crossed, would force you to break up? If so, what are they?**

The decision was so difficult because I had this Scripture ringing in the back of my head: "Therefore, if anyone is in Christ, he is a new creation; the old has gone, the new has come" (2 Corinthians 5:17). Because my boyfriend was a Christian, I felt like I should ignore everything that had happened in his past, regardless of how it might affect our future. But the verse does not say, "Therefore, if anyone is *dating*, he is a new creation." *Christ* is the key component in becoming a new creation, and I was trying to play my boyfriend's savior rather than letting Jesus be his Savior. In my attempts to be like Jesus, I ended up replacing Him.

I thought I could restore what had been broken in my boyfriend. I thought I could save him. I thought I could make it all better. I was going to be the one who restored his faith in humanity and love and God. I was going to be the one with whom he finally felt safe. In retrospect I realize this is all foolish thinking. But when you're in the middle of a relationship, you feel as though your very soul is tied up inside your boyfriend's wounds.

Have you ever cared about someone so deeply that you tried to make all his or her sadness disappear? Have you ever wanted to make life easier on someone, even if God wanted to teach that person something important through the struggle?

I consulted my parents, who graciously allowed me the space and time to make my own decision; but I remember their saying, "Take a few days and ask yourself, *Do I really want to deal with this for the rest of my life?*" I felt so torn between accepting and loving as Christ has called me to do and making an intelligent decision for my own future; but my parents were right.

Do you feel comfortable going to your parents for advice when you face a difficult decision in a relationship? Do you have someone else whom you can go to, like a pastor or a big sis?

There is a saying, "You can't see the forest for the trees." In other words, the big picture gets lost when you're concentrating on the details. I became so dead set on working things out, I never paused to decide if I actually *wanted* to work things out. But God knew what was best for me and moved my boyfriend to make that decision for me. After we tearfully broke things off, I prayed that God would teach me how to be a partner rather than a pseudosavior in my next relationship.

Are you in a relationship now that you're not sure you should be in? Can you think of someone who can help you sort things out?

Waiting

I listened to U2's "Stuck in the Moment" over and over again for weeks after I got dumped.[1] I would cry every time it came on. I wanted so badly to get unstuck from my feelings of pain. Every time I tried to get unstuck, I landed on the ground in a pile of snot and salty tears.

At the end of the song, Bono sings a very hopeful lyric. Basically, he says that even when the road is dark and rough, the moment *will* pass. I was reminded that we're only done grieving when we're *done*! That might sound overly simple, but it's so true.

Let me give you another example. Have you ever tried to bake something in a hurry? If you try to speed up the process by increasing the heat, you'll burn your biscuits (or whatever you're making). And if you stand right next to the oven, opening it every two minutes, poking it with your toothpick to see if it's done yet, you'll let all the hot air out and it will *never* be done. So you're left with one (and only one) option: to wait. If bread takes 45 minutes to bake, you can't take it out after 25 minutes and be disgruntled when it's mushy in the middle.

Have you ever tried to rush something you're cooking? Do you have any funny stories about that experience?

Do you try to hurry your emotions along when you no longer want to deal with them? Do you push them down and pretend they don't exist?

It's easy to understand the principles of waiting when we're talking about cakes and soufflés and other tangible objects. But when it comes to broken hearts, we want them fixed at microwave speed, don't we? I bet if we could actually look inside our hearts and *see* our wounded emotions, we would be a bit more patient with our healing process. And so I say, "You're only done when you're *done*!" Don't try and rush the process—you'll regret it in the end.

Scar Tissue

I believe that God created things in the natural world that parallel things in the spiritual world to help us understand them better. For example, do you know that because scar tissue is made of fibers, not skin cells, it is stronger than ordinary skin? Can you believe that?

Thinking of love as a battlefield is neither romantic nor comforting, but the scars are there, nonetheless. The reassuring part is that when we are wounded deeply, we develop scars, and scars are evidence of growth. Through the injury, we emerge stronger!

💬 **Do you feel like a seasoned warrior in the battlefields of love? If so, how have your battle scars made you stronger? If you haven't entered the battlefield yet, what can you do to protect yourself from harm?**

DIVINE WRESTLING MATCH

So Jacob was left alone, and a man wrestled with him till daybreak. When the man saw that he could not overpower him, he touched the socket of Jacob's hip so that his hip was wrenched as he wrestled with the man. Then the man said, "Let me go, for it is daybreak." But Jacob replied, "I will not let you go unless you bless me." The man asked him, "What is your name?" "Jacob," he answered. Then the man said, "Your name will no longer be Jacob, but Israel, because you have struggled with God and with men and have overcome."

Genesis 32:24-28

This Scripture is filled with mystery. Some scholars believe Jacob wrestled an angel; some even believe he wrestled God Himself. All I know is that Jacob walked with a limp the rest of his life. Because of this encounter, because of his struggle, he was forever cursed! Or was he? We would be fools to forget what also happened because of this encounter—the visitor blessed him and changed his name. He became someone else that day. And that is the hope to which I believe God wishes us to hold.

I have wrestled with God, frantically trying to get my way. When one of my boyfriends broke my heart, I prayed as hard as I ever have that God would make everything go back to normal. It never did, and that is the limp I walk with. But I also became someone else that day. Who I am now is much stronger than who I was then. We must learn to say as Job did, "Though he slay me, yet will I hope in him" (Job 13:15). In other words, even when God allows painful things to happen to us, we must choose to trust and hope that He has a much greater plan at work. Pray with me.

💬 **Do you walk with a (figurative) limp? What is it? Do you think God can use it to make you stronger? How might He use your story to help others?**

God,

sometimes I don't understand why things have to happen the way they do. I don't think I'll ever understand here on Earth; maybe when I meet You face-to-face we can talk about it. But I see how much You teach me when things go wrong, and I watch myself cling to You in tough times like I never do when the road is easy. Please help me to trust You more when You allow my heart to be broken. And please teach me how to guard my heart for Your glory so that my heart isn't broken needlessly.

So be it.

Note

1. U2, "Stuck in a Moment," *All That You Can't Leave Behind*, Interscope Records, 2000.

five: the best-kept secret

I am not saying this because I am in need, for I have learned to be content what-
ever the circumstances. I know what it is to be in need, and I know what it is to have
plenty. I have learned the secret of being content in any and every situation, whether
well fed or hungry, whether living in plenty or in want.

Philippians 4:11-12

Secrets? I *love* secrets. Well, let me tell you, this is about the best secret I've ever come to learn. This is not the kind of secret that your big brother or sister uses to taunt you, or that comes back to bite you in the rear end. It's a secret that only you can discover, but maybe I can help you out a little on your journey.

Paul knew the secret. In fact, he told his friends, the Philippians, about it in Philippians chapter 4. The secret is . . . are you ready? . . . contentment. Paul learned that even though external situations may change—sometimes for the better and sometimes for the worse—our hearts can remain joyful regardless of our circumstances.

Did you notice that Paul said that he knew what it was to be in need? He wasn't faking us out. We're not talking about a rich man in a warm coat telling a beggar in bare rags on a winter's night, "I'm cold too!" Paul *knew* need. And Paul *knew* plenty.

So what does this have to do with relationships? If we were to apply Philippians 4:11-12 to the subject of this workbook, it might go something like this: "I've sat at home alone on countless Friday and Saturday nights with no date and no one calling me on the phone. On other weekends, I've not only had dinner dates, but my lunches were booked too—all with hand-some, intelligent guys. But I have learned to have true joy whether my phone is ringing off the hook or my record is 0 for 20. My happiness does not waver whether I am dating or single, for I have learned the secret of contentment."

How would you describe what it means to be content? How do you feel about Philippians 4:11-12? Do you have the urge to say, "It's not that easy, Paul!" Or have you found a joy that transcends your dating status?

God made us relational creatures. So if our need for relationship is God-given, why does it get us into so much trouble? Why does our good and healthy *desire* so quickly turn to unhealthy *desperation* in the realm of dating? We become so hungry for connection that we end up settling for much less than we were designed for. Not settling in the sense of dating someone beneath our social status (which is ridiculous; we're all humans, all on equal ground). I'm referring to the amazing fulfillment we miss out on when we seek to put guys in God's rightful place. When you believe that the only way you'll experience happiness is if you have a man in your life, you have settled.

💬 **How do you *honestly* feel when you don't have a boyfriend? Do you enjoy your singleness or are you "on the prowl," hunting for the next victim... I mean boyfriend? Do you spend your days and nights feeling miserable that you're single?**

Most of the women I know despise their singleness. They hate being alone without a boyfriend or husband. They spend their days pining away after the idea of some guy, all the while ignoring the great gifts right under their noses. They expend every bit of their energy in desperately trying to rid themselves of this dreaded curse. The moment they end one relationship, they're off to find another. If they're not with a guy, they're out looking for one.

💬 **Do you feel better when you know someone likes you, even if the guy who likes you is a jerk? Why do you think his attention makes you feel so good?**

con•tent (adj.)—1) Reasonably happy and satisfied with the way things are; 2) Willing to accept or comply with a situation or course of action; 3) To accept or make do with something, rather than taking further action or making more demands.[1]

con•tent•ment (n.)—1) A feeling of calm satisfaction; 2) A circumstance, or a feature or characteristic of something, that gives rise to satisfaction (formal or literary).[2]

🗨 **Now, being completely honest with yourself, on a scale of 1 to 10, rank how strongly you long for attention from members of the opposite gender.**

1	2	3	4	5	6	7	8	9	10

Guys? Who Needs 'Em?   **Desperate for Attention**

Check out this chorus to a song I wrote a few years back:

> *I'm casting my line in a pond of dead fish*
> *I'm breaking "The Rules" by telling you this*
> *I'm all dressed up with nowhere to go*
> *I'm chasing them down and yelling, "Chase me!"*
> *I'm baking the bread but there's no one to eat*
> *I'm pretending not to notice, but I'm still alone.*

SECRET DANGER

There's danger in not knowing the secret. When we don't find our fulfillment and worth in God, we become susceptible to obsession. And mark my words, ladies, "*Always being available is never attractive.*" Obsession is never a reasonable substitute for love. We think that when we fall in love everything will finally feel wonderful. The problem is, *feelings* don't last forever.

I'm not going to lie to you—at first it's quite flattering when a boy is crazy about you, when he calls you all the time, when he tells you he thinks about you constantly (so constantly he can't think about anything else), when he wants to spend every free minute with you. At first it's kind of fun when he puts you on a pedestal so high that you can barely see the ground and makes you feel like you're the queen of his world. I experienced it once. It was sheer ecstasy for a season! This guy was all about *me*! Everything was done for me. My slightest feeling or comments could devastate him or make his day. I felt powerful, as if I mattered to someone. At first it felt as if I were laying my head on a soft feather-down pillow (one that smells fresh and clean like detergent, with ruffles and a fancy flower-print pillowcase on it). But after a while, I felt as if that pillow were duct taped to my face. It didn't matter how pretty or soft the pillow was, I couldn't breathe! His "love" was suffocating me.

I longed to date someone so badly that I inevitably gave up parts of my own life. I lost sight of my own dreams and just hung out with him. I suspended the things I was passionate about so that there was more time for him. We spent hours upon days upon weeks with each other.

💬 **Have you ever felt powerful because of a guy's interest in you? How did that affect your view of him? Of yourself?**

💬 **Think back to any past relationships you have had. Do you tend to maintain your own sense of self, or do you think only of your boyfriend, forgetting all your own friends, interests, dreams and goals?**

the Meltdown

This particular relationship invaded all of my personal boundaries. I began to want some space, which scared him. He felt me pulling away. I wanted to reverse the dating process that was already under way. We began to bicker. We fought all the time. It did not matter what the subject was. We were *always* intense; therefore, I was *always* exhausted. Nothing was easy to navigate. The slightest offense became unforgivable.

I can honestly say he brought out the worst in me. I found myself reacting to him in ways I'd never treated another human being. I would yell at him with my fists clenched. He would make me feel like I was going crazy. Our arguments would go round and round, like some sick Ferris wheel that would never let me off the ride. At this point you might be wondering, *Kendall, what in the world were you thinking? Why would you stay with someone who caused you such anxiety and stress?* Good question. I asked myself the same question and wrote a children's poem to explain how I felt.

Honeybee

I have a little honeybee that sits upon my shoulder;
I'll trade him for a butterfly perhaps when I am older.
At first I thought he was so cute, I chose to name him Randall;
When we would play, he'd give me all the honey I could handle.
I don't know why he got so mad one day out of the blue;
I did not mean to smash his wing under my big fat shoe.
He stung me once—oh, how it hurt; I cried myself to sleep.
He stung me twice (the little twerp); he's really not so sweet!
He stung me thrice and that is when my mother said to me,
"You'll always find a stinger where you find a honeybee."

BACK TO THE *SECRET*

This is what it boiled down to: I was petrified that there would never be another man who "loved" me the way he did. That was my motivation for staying in the relationship. I felt like a drug addict—I knew he was bad for me, but I couldn't stop. The honey (his undivided attention) was just too sweet. I never realized that what he felt toward me was not love at all but a codependent obsession. There was no distinction of time (my time, his time, time together and time apart). That's no way to have a healthy, fun relationship. If I had known the secret of contentment back then, I wouldn't have traveled so far down that road. I would have spotted the dangers and made a U-turn at the first possible intersection!

💬 **Would you stay, or have you ever stayed, in a relationship because you were afraid of being alone? Do you secretly fear that there will never be another guy who will love you the way your boyfriend does now?**

Free at Last

When I finally put words to my passive-aggressive actions, the breakup was more spectacular than any Fourth of July fireworks I've ever seen. And when it was finally over, there was nothing but smoke and darkness for many months. I vowed to myself and to God that I would never do that again.

Now when I see couples start down the road to obsessiveness, or hear them confess feelings even remotely similar to those I experienced, my only advice is, "Run. Get out of it today; don't wait until tomorrow." Most of the time, they don't want to hear that—I sure didn't. But my hope is that if you're in an unhealthy relationship, as I was, you'll learn from my mistake.

You see, a relationship must be big enough to incorporate *all* of you, not just *parts* of you. My career and personal time was threatening to my boyfriend, and so I had to check those parts of my personality at the door. I became less of me in order to survive in relationship with him. Now I know that the miracle of marriage is not taking half-a-person and another half-a-person to make a whole person. God's desire is to take one *whole* person and another *whole* person, join them together and proclaim Ephesians 5:31: "And the two will become one flesh." Now that's a miracle!

💬 Are you the type of person to be honest about the pitfalls and potentially negative aspects of a relationship? If several of your friends and family came to you and told you that they had serious concerns about your relationship, would you listen? Why or why not?

FOUND
WHAT I'M LOOKING FOR

There's a song by U2 called "I Still Haven't Found What I'm Looking For."[3] In my humble opinion, it sounds strangely similar to Philippians 4:11. Here's my rough paraphrase of the lyrics, "I have climbed the highest mountains, swum the deepest seas and crawled through burning deserts, but I still haven't found the secret of contentment, because I have done all these things only to be with you—my ever-elusive relationship. I did these things, not for myself or for my God, but only to be with you."

Jesus puts the "secret" in the secret of contentment. He fills the void. *He* is what we are looking for. In our desperation for completion, we turn to human relationships rather than finding satisfaction from the source.

Do you want contentment? I know no other way to find it than to ask the secret holder. Let's pray.

Father,

You know all things and I know so little. I don't know how to be happy alone. I don't know how to feel true joy and satisfaction without a love interest on my horizon. Tell me the secret. Teach me Your ways, that I might walk in Your truth. So be it.

Notes
1. *Encarta World English Dictionary*. Developed for Microsoft by Bloomsbury Publishing Plc., 1999, s.v. "content."
2. Ibid., s.v. "contentment."
3. U2, "I Still Haven't Found What I'm Looking For," *Joshua Tree*, 1987.

six: He feels like home

I write in my journal often, and sometimes I forget what I've written. Every once in a while I'll flip through my notebook and stumble upon a minefield of great thoughts days, weeks, months, sometimes even years after the original thoughts took shape.

💬 Do you journal? If not, why? Are you afraid it won't come out right? Are you afraid someone will read it? Are you afraid you don't have anything to say? Or do you just not feel you have the time?

💬 If you already journal, what is your favorite topic or style of writing? Do you do it just to vent and get things off your chest? Or do you do it to organize your thoughts and better understand yourself?

on belonging

Writing not only allows us to capture the feelings of a moment, but it also helps us solidify our thoughts. Sometimes while I'm writing, something I've been wrestling with will suddenly become as clear as day. That's why writing can play such an important role in your quest for love. Expressing your thoughts, dreams, observations and expectations about dating and love will help you become wise. Years down the road, looking back at those journal entries will help you gain perspective.

I recently found this journal entry that I thought was just a throwaway writing exercise. But when I reread it, I was deeply moved by the beauty of innocence and love that it captured. I hope you are too.

He Feels Like Home to Me

There is this marvelous clanging of a drainpipe being dripped upon just outside my window. It reminds me that it rained today. I can sense the cold air even while snuggled up in my bed covers, and in my mind I can still see the wet streets and sidewalks covered with brown fallen leaves. I may not have fancy cars, expensive clothes or a multitude of friends, but I have the rhythmic pulse of a leftover rain shower to keep me company. That, and the thought of him, is enough for me tonight. . .

Yesterday marked the first rain of the season, and I was with him. We stood on the front porch at a party and awaited the storm. He also loves the rain, but not as much as I do. The first drops fell and the smell of the wet pavement began to make me giddy. I told him all my memories of rain; he is such a good listener.

We stared at the sky, waiting patiently as the clouds rolled in—dark, thunderous storm clouds. I thought back to the last time we stood gazing up into the universe. It was on the Fourth of July. We had decided at the last minute to try and find a fireworks display. We drove through a curvy canyon out to the beach with a group of friends. When we got down to the water's edge, the explosions began. You could see them reflecting off the water in red, purple and gold. He saw me squeal and giggle, jumping up and down. I felt like a child, and for the most part, I acted like one. I couldn't help myself. The explosions above echoed my own feelings, a mirror in the sky that revealed my truest soul. My heart was on fire along with the heavens. He just never knew my excitement was because of him.

Fire in the sky is one thing, but what can compare with the smell and sight of a well-lit fireplace? I built a blazing fire, with real logs. It was wonderful until I had to open the door for fear of smoke poisoning. I'm not exactly a Boy Scout. I sort of smoked myself out. And as I went to open it, I found a spider web hanging in the upper right-hand corner of the window. The rain left little drops of water on the many strands. It looked like a lace web, like something a bride would wear on her wedding day. I think of my wedding day, which is only a figment of my imagination for now. But I smile, knowing it will be a reality one day.

The chill of the storm hangs in the air and blows slowly and silently in through the crack at my door. I am drinking something warm and it makes me feel like Christmas morning. How can it feel like Christmas when it is in fact not Christmas? Maybe Christmas is not a day. Maybe Christmas is a feeling of happiness, warmth, family and traditions. I keep trying desperately to explain the feeling I have right now. I am sure if I could bottle it up and sell it for a penny, I'd be a millionaire by midnight. The fire crackles and I feel alive inside. The romance of life is overwhelming me. My romance with him is everything I dreamed it could be. Home, they say, is where the heart is. I guess I finally feel at home now that I'm with him.

home (n.)—1) Where somebody was born or raised or feels he or she belongs; 2) The place where something is most common or indigenous, or where something had its origins; 3) A place where a person or animal can find refuge and safety or live in security.[1]

be•long (v.)—1) To be linked to a particular place or person by a relationship such as birth, affection, or membership; 2) To be a part or component of something else; 3) To be accepted or made welcome in a place or group.[2]

We all yearn to belong. That's one of the reasons why we so desperately want to be in relationships with guys. We want to belong to someone, to feel we matter to someone, to know there is another human being who cherishes us. We don't have to feel ashamed of this desire. In fact, God Himself gave us the desire to be loved.

PASSION AND DESIRE

Here's another journal entry, but first a word of caution: This one gets a little steamy!

My lover is mine and I am His. Restless in bed and sleepless through the night, I longed for my lover. I wanted him desperately. His absence was painful. You've captured my heart, dear friend. You looked at me, and I fell in love. One look my way and I was hopelessly in love! How beautiful your love, dear, dear friend—far more pleasing than a fine, rare wine, your fragrance more exotic than select spices. The kisses of your lips are honey, my love, every syllable you speak a delicacy to savor.... Dear lover and friend, you're a secret garden, a private and pure fountain. Body and soul, you are paradise. I beg you.... if you find my lover, please tell him I want him, that I'm heartsick with love for him.... My dear lover glows with health—red-blooded, radiant! He's one in a million. There's no one quite like him! My golden one, pure and untarnished.... His eyes are like doves, soft and bright, but deep-set, brimming with meaning, like wells of water. His face is rugged, his beard smells like sage, his voice, his words, warm and reassuring. Fine muscles ripple beneath his skin, quiet and beautiful. His torso is the work of a sculptor, hard and smooth as ivory.... His words are kisses, his kisses words. Everything about him delights me, thrills me through and through! That's my lover, that's my man. The feelings I get when I see the high mountain ranges—stirrings of desire, longings for the heights—remind me of you, and I'm spoiled for anyone else! Your beauty, within and without, is absolute, dear lover, close companion. I am my lover's. I'm all he wants. I am all the world to him! Come, dear lover—let's tramp through the countryside. Let's sleep at some wayside inn, then rise early and listen to bird-song. Let's look for wildflowers in bloom, blackberry bushes blossoming white, fruit trees festooned with cascading flowers. And there I'll give myself to you, my love to your love!

Are you blushing yet? All that talk of tramping through the countryside and sleeping at a wayside inn sounds a little risqué to me! But I didn't write it! In fact, if you open your Bible to a book called Song of Songs (sometimes called Song of Solomon) you'll find this soul-baring dialogue between a young married couple (Song of Solomon 2:11; 3:1-2; 4:9-13; 5:8-16; 7:5-6,10-12, *The Message*). God does not want us to be ashamed of our desire to fall madly in love. He wants us to enjoy the feelings He has given us. It's right there in His book! Scripture speaks openly about passion and romance and about the thrill of enjoying both in the right context and at the right time.

🗨 **Have you ever read Song of Songs? When you think about romance, passion and love, do you leave God out of the equation? Do you view your sexuality and desires as God's inventions or as things Satan uses to pull you away from God?**

the bare necessities

Have you ever played the Desert Island game? It goes something like this: If you were trapped on a desert island and had a moment to grab a few things before you left the house (knowing you were going to be stranded), what would you take? There are many variations of this game: the five books you'd bring, the three people you'd bring—you get the point.

Okay, so now imagine a Desert Island game in which you have to choose the 10 most important qualities in your future spouse. What would those be? Mine goes something like this:

1. Mature faith
2. Strong personality
3. Sense of humor
4. Intelligent
5. Attractive
6. Extrovert
7. Driven
8. Talkative
9. Independent
10. Tall—must be tall!

Now it's your turn. Write down the 10 most essential qualities that you desire for your future husband.

1.

2.

3.

4.

5.

6.

7.

8.

9.

10.

I want you to keep this list. I hope you've looked into the future as well as the present and written real desires, not just the things you *should* say. Then, when you find a guy that interests you, I want you to pull out this list and see if he meets the criteria.

Of course, remember that God is full of surprises. We are all works in progress, so if this guy is painfully lacking a few items but has the most important qualities (faith, respect, etc.) going for him, don't drop him like a hot potato. *Talk to him about it!* It might be something he's never realized about himself. He might be overjoyed to work on that area of his life. You just never know!

💬 Now I want you to think about *you*. **What do you think a good guy is looking for in a girl? (And don't say "big boobs and a tight butt." I asked what a "good" guy is looking for. A quality guy values much more than that!)**

1.

2.

3.

4.

5.

6.

7.

8.

9.

10.

💬 **What are you doing to become the kind of woman you just described? What else can you do? If you're not sure, ask God to show you.**

If you want to be with the kind of man you described in your list, you have to become someone he finds attractive spiritually, emotionally and intellectually. God wants to give his daughters *good* gifts (see James 1:17). He wants to see you fulfilled by a healthy, mature, passionate relationship—*when the time is right*. Are you willing to trust *His* timing? Let's pray.

God,

teach me what to look for in a man, and help me become the kind of woman You desire me to be. Give me wisdom and insight in my dating relationships. Please prepare someone for me who will show me new dimensions of Your glory. Help me recognize him when the time is right.

So be it.

Notes
1. *Encarta World English Dictionary*. Developed for Microsoft by Bloomsbury Publishing, 1999, s.v. "home."
2. Ibid., s.v. "belong."

part two:
friends

seven:
dealing with the obvious

Friends—the word conjures up a multitude of images. Monica, Rachel, Phoebe, Joey, Chandler and Ross for starters! Then I see a bunch of youth-group kids sitting around a campfire with linked arms singing, "And a friend's a friend forever . . . "

In the next six chapters, we'll talk about what to look for in a friend; but more important, I want God to change you and make *you* into a good friend. You must first become the kind of friend you are looking for, and then I'm sure you'll find one.

What is a friend to you? Who are your friends? What do you guys talk about when you get together? You're going to have lots of space to tell me how you feel, so get out your pen and let's get started!

THE PINK ELEPHANT

My friend has a big pink elephant that sits in the middle of her living room. It's enormous! It probably weighs six tons. The sheer enormity of the animal makes it impossible to miss. But everyone ignores it and pretends everything's normal. Can you imagine how silly people look when they come over to visit? They have to walk all the way around the room to avoid bumping into the elephant. But no one talks about it, and no one asks my friend to take her animal to the circus where it belongs.

When I first met my friend I was totally unaware that she had this monstrosity in the middle of her living room. So who could blame me for exclaiming at the top of my lungs upon first sight of the beast, "Oh my goodness! Why is there a big pink elephant in the middle of your living room?" Leave it to me to state the obvious!

As you can imagine, my question did not go over too well. Some people live their whole lives in denial, and they expect others to humor them by looking the other way. These people are not so keen on being reminded of reality, and they become especially displeased with the people who administer those reminders.

So you've probably guessed that my friend didn't literally have a six-ton elephant in her living room, let alone one of a pink persuasion. Have you ever heard the term "pink elephant"? The phrase describes those things we don't want to see in our own lives. We should deal with them, but that takes too much effort, so we ignore them even though everyone around us sees them as plain as day.

We all have pink elephants that sit in the living rooms of our souls. They are our insecurities. They are the unresolved issues from childhood. They are our selfish attitudes. They are the skeletons in our closets. My friend's pink elephant was jealousy. She had always wanted to be the prettiest and most popular girl in her circle. Of course, she'd never ever say that out loud, but she would subtly try and keep her friends down so that she could rise to the top, all the while appearing to be very loving. Well, when I met her, I sensed that bent toward jealousy right away and I just flat out told her. Like I said, it was not the finest hour of our friendship!

When we invite people into our space—into our lives—our problems and flaws can become obvious to them. But because we don't want to acknowledge our shortcomings, we banish them to secret chambers in our hearts, refusing to discuss them with anyone. Others opt not to say anything about your elephants for fear that you might point out theirs. So we tiptoe around each other's enormous elephants and pretend they don't exist.

We will never be comfortable in our own skin until we're willing to see these elephants in our own lives.

I do admit that I have fears that when I come you'll disappoint me and I'll disappoint you, and in frustration with each other everything will fall to pieces—quarrels, jealousy, flaring tempers, taking sides, angry words, vicious rumors, swelled heads, and general bedlam. I don't look forward to a second humiliation by God among you (2 Corinthians 12:20-21, The Message).

> 💬 Do any of your friends fit this description? Have you ever tried to talk to her about these issues? What was your friend's reaction?

> 💬 What issues in your heart and life do you pretend don't exist? This question might be hard to answer at first, because you're probably still pretending! But just take a moment to ask the Holy Spirit to gently show you whatever you need to see.

Now you have to admit, Paul was pretty honest in this letter to his friends. I love that he told it like it is! He admitted that he was afraid they were going to disappoint him, but that they would be disappointed with him too. It takes guts to admit people might not be as impressed with you as you'd like them to be. And he spoke candidly about his fear that God would humble him in front of everyone. He was afraid he'd look like a fool—who isn't afraid of that? He openly pointed out his pink elephants so that no one had to tiptoe around them and so that his friends could keep him accountable. It's a beautiful thing when two friends can be that honest with each other! But it can be very scary at first. You risk rejection and embarrassment.

mirror, mirror
on the wall...

I want you to do an experiment for me. I want you to count how many times in the course of a day you find yourself in front of a mirror either checking yourself out or just walking by one. Then I want you to recognize how you feel before and after you see your reflection. Write down your findings below.

Can you imagine life without mirrors? Can you imagine *your* life without a mirror anywhere in the world? Think about that for a second.

I attended a party once where the guest list consisted of models, actors and just plain ol' beautiful people. I don't know why they invited me! I felt fine on the doorstep ringing the doorbell. I was feeling pretty confident and comfortable with myself. But crossing the threshold I realized very quickly the caliber of attractiveness jam-packed in this tiny apartment. Like a trapped animal, I frantically searched for the mirror, desperate to reevaluate my outfit, haircut and color of lipstick. I had to see if I was "cool enough" to be at this party. And then a strange thought hit me.

Everyone else could see me plainly. It was *I* who couldn't see me. The mirror was invented for *me*, and for all the people in the world who want to see what others see. And then another strange thought hit me. If God, in all his infinite wisdom, wanted us to be able to see ourselves (as others do), He would have given us eyeballs on the end of long tentacles like aliens!

When I think about how unnatural it is to behold our own faces, I think that God might have had a purpose in His design plan. (He's so sneaky!) What other purpose does a mirror serve than to remind me of *me*? It seems too familiar to even comprehend life without looking at yourself, but imagine this if you can: a world without mirrors. What would it be like? If we weren't reminded of ourselves around every corner, would we think about others more often?

💬 **Have you ever thought about asking God to tell you how beautiful you are instead of needing to see it in a mirror? Do you think you could try that next time?**

LESSONS FROM A
greek hottie

If we weren't able to see our own beauty, would we be freed to admire others' beauty? Would we compare our looks to theirs? If we weren't able to see that big piece of green spinach stuck between our teeth, would we take ourselves a little less seriously and laugh more often? Or would we gather around lakes, ponds and any still waters we could find to bask in our own splendor?

Have you heard the story of Narcissus? In a nutshell, this really handsome Greek guy (Narcissus) saw his reflection in a crystal clear fountain when he stooped down to take a drink. He became so enamored with his own reflection—fell so in love with himself—that he forgot to eat or sleep. He just sat there at the water's edge and fawned over his chiseled face! The myth purports that he sat there so long that he eventually lost his youthful good looks.

💬 **What lesson can we learn from Narcissus?**

The very eyes I use to behold every other face disallow me to see my own face. I believe there is a deep spiritual lesson to be learned here.

I heard a story about a woman who rid her whole house of mirrors, not an image of herself to be found. I thought that would be a wonderful idea, until I realized I'd have no clue what I looked like walking out the door every day. I was terrified that I would look unattractive and that people would judge me on how I looked.

I've always considered myself a deep person; I don't stay shallow for too long in any of my friendships. But when I look in the mirror, I see a big pink elephant staring back at me. I have to face the fact that I *do* care so much about my appearance. I care about how I appear to other people, which also means that I am sizing them up, deciding if I think they're attractive enough to be my friend. Oh, I know it's awful! But I'm at least willing to look at it and deal with it. I hope you are too!

💬 **Dust off your dictionary and look up the word "narcissistic." Do you know any people you'd describe that way? What bothers you the most about them? How do those people make you feel when you're around them?**

💬 **What main criteria do you use when choosing friends? Must they look a certain way? Must they hold a certain social status? Do you care if they have messy or dirty hair? Do you care if they wear their mom's hand-me-downs from 1960? Do you care if they have warts and pimples? Be honest!**

THE BEAUTY
OF KINDNESS

A friend loves at all times, and a brother is born for adversity.

Proverbs 17:17

Love is patient, love is kind. It does not envy, it does not boast, it is not proud. It is not

rude, it is not self-seeking, it is not easily angered, it keeps no record of wrongs.

Love does not delight in evil but rejoices with the truth. It always protects, always

trusts, always hopes, always perseveres.

1 Corinthians 13:4-7

Think back to when you were a little girl—maybe five or six years old. Did you care if your best friend wore mismatched socks? Did you care if her ponytail didn't remain in perfect placement on her head? Did you care about what she looked like in a bathing suit standing next to you? No! You cared about having *fun*! You spent time with whatever friends you had the most fun with. Somewhere in the growing-up process we forfeit "fun" for "status." When you choose a friend based on who gives you the greatest ego boost, you will always choose poorly. Let me just tell you straight up—it's a terrible way to live. And though we all find ourselves there at some point in life, I pray your transition will be fast and furious!

💬 **List three of your closest friends. Write about what makes them so special to you. What have they taught you about life and love and God? What do you think you've taught them? If you're comfortable enough, share the list with them.**

When I was 15 years old, I met my first best friend. Out of all the lessons she taught me, one of the greatest was to be *kind*. This might be a no-brainer to those of you who are naturally kind. But I'm not the kindest person around! (I think it's actually a genetic defect.) If you want to vent and share your emotions, go somewhere else! But, if you want *painfully* honest advice (notice I stressed the painful part!), you can knock on my door morning, noon or night. It sounds awful, but it's true!

I embody the classic your-greatest-strength-is-also-your-greatest-weakness principle. I am, for the most part, unemotional about my decisions. And when the job needs to get done, I don't care if people's feelings get hurt along the way. In my little warped brain, the end always justifies the means. What I never realized was how cruel I could seem to others.

Fortunately for me, God seems to bless us with people who naturally soften our hard edges and build us up where we are weak. It just so happened that my first real friendship was with someone who did not have a mean bone in her body. She always assisted people when they asked for help, even when it was physically or emotionally impossible for her. I often joked that the reason I was her friend was to teach her that saying no was okay and that the reason she was my friend was to teach me that saying yes would not kill me.

As long as I'm being honest, I also tend to lean toward selfishness. Most of the time, if something isn't convenient for me, I'm not going to do it! So at 15 years old, I watched in astonishment as my new friend would bend over backward to meet the needs of others, sometimes even to her own discomfort! Can you believe it? Offer myself to another human being, without asking first what benefit I could gain? Well, it was groundbreaking news to me!

Kindness draws someone *in* instead of pushing them *out*. Kindness considers the feelings of others; it empathizes with their pain and sorrow. In time (and with my friend's persistency), I began to realize that I didn't like the person I was. I asked God to change my heart, and sure enough, He did! I started to care about people who hadn't meant anything to me. I started to care about their stories as if they were my own. When someone needed an ear or a hand, I started to listen or help. The joy that followed was incredible! I found that by giving, I was truly receiving.

💬 **Do you consider yourself a kind person? Do you only care about your close friends, or do you show kindness to everyone who needs help or a listening ear?**

Will you pray this with me?

God,

I want to see the pink elephants in my own life, but I need Your grace because I can't do it on my own. Please give me friends who will walk this journey alongside me, and who will teach me about myself and about You. I want to become strong in the areas in which I'm weak. And I want my immaturities to grow into maturity. Please continue to change me through my friends and teach me to be a better friend for them. I thank You for their friendship.

So be it.

I've always had three types of friends. First, I have a friendship with a mentor—a woman who is older and wiser than I am, but whom I can laugh with and relate to. Next I have a peer friendship—someone close to my age and at a similar life stage. Finally, I always choose someone younger than I am into whom I can pour some of my life lessons. I have a real friendship with this young woman, but it's more about my giving and less about my receiving.

💬 **Do you have friendships in any (or each) of these categories (someone you learn from, someone you journey with and someone you pour into)? Tell me about them. If you don't already have these relationships in place, how can you work on finding people who will fulfill these rolls?**

words of wisdom

My son, if you accept my words and store up my commands within you, turning your ear to wisdom and applying your heart to understanding, and if you call out for insight and cry aloud for understanding, and if you look for it as for silver and search for it as for hidden treasure, then you will understand the fear of the Lord and find the knowledge of God. For the Lord gives wisdom, and from his mouth come knowledge and understanding.
Proverbs 2:1-6

Wisdom is a good thing, wouldn't you agree? I'd take being wise over being a fool any day. But how do we get wisdom? Well, we can read Scripture. We can pray and receive it directly from God through impressions on our hearts. But God also allows us to attain wisdom through spiritual mentors, or "big sisses," He places in our paths. Through what seem like random circumstances (the place you were born, schools you attended, the kids you've baby-sat, etc.), God allows us to meet and bond with people who become responsible for our spiritual growth.

💬 **Do you have a mentor? Do you see the need for one in your life? Who has been the greatest influence on your spiritual life thus far?**

The story of Ruth and Naomi is a beautiful example of friendship between a younger woman and an older woman. The story begins with a famine that forces a woman named Naomi—who is married and has two sons—to travel from Moab back to Judah.

> *Now Elimelech, Naomi's husband, died, and she was left with her two sons. They married Moabite women, one named Orpah and the other Ruth. After they had lived there about ten years, both Mahlon and Kilion also died, and Naomi was left without her two sons and her husband* (Ruth 1:3-5).

Time out. Can you imagine the grief these women went through? Naomi lost her husband and two sons, and both Orpah and Ruth lost their husbands. They had nothing left in the world, except each other.

> *Then Naomi said to her two daughters-in-law, "Go back, each of you, to your mother's home. May the Lord show kindness to you, as you have shown to your dead and to me. May the Lord grant that each of you will find rest in the home of another husband"* (Ruth 1:8-9).

The women wept bitterly because they loved Naomi and they didn't want to say good-bye. Orpah decided that it was best to return home, leaving her sister- and mother-in-law. But Ruth clung to Naomi.

> *"Look," said Naomi, "your sister-in-law is going back to her people and her gods. Go back with her." But Ruth replied, "Don't urge me to leave you or to turn back from you. Where you go I will go, and where you stay I will stay. Your people will be my people and your God my God. Where you die I will die, and there I will be buried. May the Lord deal with me, be it ever so severely, if anything but death separates you and me"* (Ruth 1:15-17).

Ruth's love for her mother-in-law is a stellar example of holding on with all our might to the mentors God places in our lives with all our might. You should never allow distance or business to interrupt these special friendships—you must commit to the friendship. This hits close to home for me because my mentor is moving from America to Europe next year. An ocean will separate our physical bodies, but that won't matter. Our hearts will always be connected.

kindred *spirits*

The second kind of friendship is a lateral friendship—a friendship with your peers. These are friends who walk beside you on your journey; people who wrestle with the same issues that you do on a daily basis and are willing to talk about their victories *and* defeats. These friends may not always know the answers, but they are always willing to grapple with the questions beside you.

Which friends do you share everyday life with? What are your favorite qualities in them? What would you sacrifice for them, if anything?

The Bible tells a marvelous story about this kind of friendship. First a little background. The great King David was once a poor shepherd boy who happened to be at the right place at the right time. He picked up a slingshot and hurled a stone through space, planting it directly in the center of a giant's forehead. (If you don't know the story of David and Goliath, I recommend you check it out! You'll find it in 1 Samuel 17.) Needless to say, this act of bravery caught King Saul's attention. The king was so impressed, he wouldn't let David go home; instead he insisted that David come live at his house, the castle. Now you tell me, what poor shepherd boy would say no to that? And it's a good thing he said yes, because that was where he first met Jonathan (Saul's son—next in line for the throne). Here's what took place between them:

> *After David had finished talking with Saul, Jonathan became one in spirit with David, and he loved him as himself. From that day Saul kept David with him and did not let him return to his father's house. And Jonathan made a covenant with David because he loved him as himself. Jonathan took off the robe he was wearing and gave it to David, along with his tunic, and even his sword, his bow and his belt* (1 Samuel 18:1-4).

Talk about kindred spirits! They were best friends from the get-go. But like all good friendships, their bond had to be tested through fire.

King Saul became increasingly jealous of David (the giant-killing shepherd boy). The king was so enraged with envy that he wanted David dead! But Dave was a smart guy, and he picked up on the assassination plan and told his best bud Jonathan, who of course didn't want to believe his father could ever stoop so low. So Dave and Jon concocted a plan that would allow Jonathan to warn David if it was true. Here's how it went: Dave was supposed to have dinner with King Saul, but Jonathan went instead. They figured that if Saul didn't care that Dave wasn't there, then all was cool. But Jon knew that if Saul got mad, Dave was a goner. On to the dinner scene . . .

> Saul's anger flared up at Jonathan and he said to him, "You son of a perverse and rebellious woman! Don't I know that you have sided with the son of Jesse to your own shame and to the shame of the mother who bore you? As long as the son of Jesse lives on this earth, neither you nor your kingdom will be established. Now send and bring him to me, for he must die!" "Why should he be put to death? What has he done?" Jonathan asked his father. But Saul hurled his spear at him to kill him. Then Jonathan knew that his father intended to kill David (1 Samuel 20:30-32).

Talk about a dysfunctional family! Yikes! Can you imagine your dad trying to kill your best friend and then trying to kill you too? That's a little more than I could handle. Now let's talk about what Jonathan was giving up by opposing his father and letting David live. He was giving up his *right to the throne*. He was giving up his destiny to become king himself!

That would be like you and your best friend both being nominated for homecoming queen (except way more intense). And you know that you're going to win, so you decide to pull out of the race so that your friend will be crowned.

💬 **What would you do if you were in Jonathan's shoes? Can you imagine loving a friend so much that you would really want the best for her, even if it meant you got the bum end of the deal?**

Back to our story. Now that Jonathan knew the truth, he had to warn David. They met secretly in a field so that Jon could give Dave the news.

David got up from the south side of the stone and bowed down before Jonathan three times, with his face to the ground. Then they kissed each other and wept together—but David wept the most. Jonathan said to David, "Go in peace, for we have sworn friendship with each other in the name of the Lord, saying, 'The Lord is witness between you and me, and between your descendants and my descendants forever'" (1 Samuel 20:41-42).

It turns out blood is not *always* thicker than water!

I think one of the finest literary and cinematic examples of this kind of friendship comes from *The Lord of the Rings* trilogy. Samwise Gamgee is Frodo's best friend. There are too many moments to recount here, but one of the greatest comes at the end of *The Return of the King*, when the two hobbits stop halfway up the mountain in utter exhaustion. Their lips are bubbling from blisters, their faces are caked in mud, and their clothes are nothing more than rags. The burden of being the ring bearer is more than Frodo can handle. When all apparent strength has failed and all hope is lost, Sam makes a statement that reveals the heart of a true friend. He says to Frodo (referring to the ring), "I cannot carry it for you, but I *can* carry *you*!" And with that he picks up his friend's limp, lifeless body and continues up the mountain.

Not only do we need those kinds of friends in our lives, but we also need to be those kinds of friends for others.

When your friends need you most, do you give all of yourself? Brainstorm some ways that you can be there for your friends in their times of need. (Maybe you could go so far as to ask them point-blank, "How can I be a better friend to you when times get tough?")

giving **back**

Finally we come to the last type of friendship—one with someone younger than you. Most times, even though you think you're going to teach her something about life and God, you end up *receiving* more than you bargained for!

Paul felt this way about Timothy. He referred to him as "my son" and bragged about Timothy's devotion to God (1 Corinthians 4:17). Paul was proud of Timothy's decisions and heart. He told the Philippians, "I have no one else like [Timothy], who takes a genuine interest in your welfare" (Philippians 2:20). (If you want to read more about this relationship, check out 1 and 2 Timothy.)

I have three younger girls with whom I spend time on a regular basis. After five years of sharing our lives together, we have countless legendary stories that we love to recount over and over. Sometimes we have sleepovers; sometimes we stop and get milk shakes and talk until we can't talk anymore. The key is to have lots of fun and to just let them catch glimpses of your life. They will learn by your example, so make sure the example you're setting is one they should follow. As your relationships with these younger girls grow, they will know who to call when they have something they need to talk about.

> Think of a few young girls who might need a little of your attention. In the space provided, write down a couple fun and memorable things that you could do with them. Call them up and invite them (but you'll want to ask their parents first). I promise it will mean the world to them!

The circle will continue as these younger girls grow up and begin investing their lives into other girls. Think of it as a way to thank God for the big sisses and mentors He has placed in your life. Pray with me.

Father,
I know You've given us a world jam-packed with people for a purpose, and You've given us the gift of friendship that makes life so much sweeter. Teach me how to be intentional about my friendships; lead me, by Your mercy, to the right kinds of people.
So be it.

nine: waterproof mascara

Sometimes you need a friend who will laugh with you until you cry. And sometimes you need a friend who will cry with you until you laugh. Whatever the emotional state, you're going to need some waterproof mascara. So the way I see it, the best combination is a friend you can cry with, laugh with *and* shop for makeup with!

What are your favorite places to shop? What sort of makeup do you like best (if you wear makeup)?

What are your favorite things to do when you and your friends hang out? Shop? Eat? Watch movies? Do you ever have *meaningful* conversations? Do you share your struggles and secrets, or do you mostly talk about surface stuff?

A FRIEND FOR
ALL SEASONS

There is a time for everything, and a season for every activity under heaven:
a time to weep and a time to laugh, a time to mourn and a time to dance,
a time to scatter stones and a time to gather them, a time to embrace
and a time to refrain, a time to search and a time to give up . . .
a time to be silent and a time to speak.
Ecclesiastes 3:1,4-7

God has given us specific seasons of the soul. I believe He also gives us specific friends to help us weather those seasons.

💬 **Can you recall any specific season in your life when it seemed God gave you a friend specifically for that time? Use this journal space to tell me about it.**

When I was 15, I was a little—how shall we say?—awkward. (Some might call it "fashion challenged," but that sounds a bit harsh, don't you think?) I didn't have a clue what kind of makeup to buy, and even if I did, I didn't know where it was supposed to go on my face. I ended up looking like a clown most of the time. I had never plucked a single eyebrow. I had never learned to use a straightening iron. I didn't even know what a "hair product" was. And I definitely didn't know how to dress! I think I owned one pair of shoes, and I wore them with *everything!*

My best friend had a sense of style like nobody's business. The very first Christmas we celebrated as friends, she brought me a goody bag of cosmetic essentials. Her gift meant so much to me that I still think about it with fond memories a decade later. She taught me how to be girly—not a prissy, stuck-up, can't-go-out-of-the-house-without-makeup girly, but classically feminine. She showed me how to contour my shadows and thin out my brow line. She fixed my hair just right and lightened my shade of lip gloss. I learned then that a real friend sees your beauty inside and does not feel threatened when it starts to shine on the outside. In fact, a true friend will encourage your success and not smother it.

💬 **If your friend were to ask you what she should wear tonight when you go out with a group of friends, how would you respond?**

A. I'd tell her to wear that lime green Sesame Street Muppet-looking sweater (the one that makes her look sick, pale and fat).

B. I'd probably say, "I dunno. Ask someone else."

C. I'd encourage her to wear the cute new outfit she got last week (the one that fits her just right and is a perfect color for her complexion).

Woolly Sweaters and
ROLLER-COASTER RIDES

I have a confession: I give feelings to inanimate objects. I know it's a little weird, but then again, I never claimed I was normal. For example, I got a new computer, and when I'd put it into sleep mode, I'd try and be very quiet so I wouldn't disturb its slumber! How strange is that? But it gets even *more* fun when I start describing my friends by using inanimate objects. One of my friends is a big, woolly sweater. In other words, I wrap myself up in her when I feel that my days have turned bitter cold. Another friend feels like a cold glass of lemonade on a hot summer's day. When I am weary and worn, I call her and immediately feel pepped up. Another friend feels like a roller-coaster ride—I just get in the cage and hang on for dear life! There's never a dull moment when she's around.

This is what makes each and every one of my friends so dear and special. Like the old saying, "Make new friends but keep the old. One is silver and the other's gold." Each friend brings out a different side of my personality. Each one awakes a part of me that lies dormant in her absence.

> Now it's your turn. Using familiar objects, describe your three best friends. To get started, ask yourself, *When do I go to this friend? What specific purpose does this friend serve in my life?* (You're going to have to get really creative on this one! Don't skip it though, it will be fun!)

LAUGH OFTEN
AND MUCH

Knowing how to laugh hard and often is a core value in friendship for me. Friends should laugh together as often as possible. When we laugh, we forget to take everything so seriously. We remember that life is too short to waste it on seemingly important things that really aren't so important. When we laugh, we let our guards down and let people enter in.

One of the funniest friendships of my life evolved because of pitiful, broken love lives. My friend and I each had been dating our boyfriend for more than a year, and within just a few weeks of each other we were both relationshipless (I prefer this term to "dumped;" somehow it sounds a little less embarrassing). Those days are a blur of ice cream, bitterness and sidesplitting laughter.

I remember one night we took a trip to Baskin-Robbins. Mint chocolate chip was her weapon of choice. I opted for some fudgy, swirly, chunky, chocolate thing, made with a sugar substitute instead of the real stuff (as if that made it justifiable).

We sat on her bed, rehashing memories of how our exes had treated us wrong and consoling each other. After we had talked about as long as we could stand, I headed home with a full belly, a full heart and a smile on my face.

Much later that evening, when I crawled into bed, I felt an odd sensation in my lower abdomen. After about an hour of pretending to be the queen upon my throne (if you catch my drift!), I finally made it back to bed. When I awoke the next morning, the previous evening's fiasco was a distant (but all too painful) memory.

About four or five days later I was on the phone with my friend. She sheepishly asked me, "Did you have any intestinal issues the other night after our ice-cream extravaganza? Because my night didn't end for a while!" She went on to tell me all about her night, which made mine seem rather mild, and with the luxury of hindsight, every detail seemed *hilarious!*

Upon hearing her story, I laughed harder than I've ever laughed in my life. We told this story over and over to everyone we met, and it didn't matter if they laughed or thought we were disgusting because it was *our* special memory.

Do you have any funny memories from sleep overs, birthday parties or school functions? What makes you laugh harder than anything in this world? *Who* makes you laugh more than anyone in this world?

when the laughter stops

Another night was a different story entirely. I had just exited a movie theater. As I walked to my parking space, a car pulled up right next to me. At first I was alarmed. It approached me so fast and came so close it nearly hit me. But once I recognized it, and realized it was my dear friend, I calmed down. I thought she was playing a joke on me. I thought she was going to say "Ha-ha! You should have seen your face!" But as soon as the tinted window rolled down, I realized something was terribly wrong.

In rapid-fire statements she said, "I've been driving for three hours and I can't find my sister anywhere! I saw your truck here and thought maybe she was with you. I've been waiting for you . . . " And then the sobbing began.

I opened the car door and held her as tightly as I could. Her body was shaking. She managed to get out, "This isn't like her. She doesn't do things like this. She always tells me where she's going. What if something's happened?" And then the tears started again.

I left my car there, knowing she was in no condition to drive, and I took her home. I put on a pot of coffee and told her over and over that things were going to be fine. It wasn't even midnight yet. Her sister must have encountered some last-minute plans and just forgot to leave a note. We waited another hour.

If you've ever sat near a window, trying desperately to not let your mind go to worst-case scenarios, you know that every headlight you see brings your heart up into your throat. And every time it drives past your driveway, your heart plummets into your stomach. She didn't want to call their parents and worry them if nothing was wrong, but her fuse was running short and she wanted some answers soon. I told her we would wait another hour and then we'd call the police. The hour came and went.

Finally, we called 911. She informed them of the situation and described her sister's vehicle. Immediately she went as cold as stone and her eyes became as round as full moons. I caught her body as her legs gave out from underneath her and she crumpled into my arms. The phone fell to the ground and she cried out, "There's been an accident! My sister's in the hospital!"

💬 **Describe your emotions right now. Who would you want around you to "catch your fall" if you had to hear life-altering news? What makes those people and friends so special and dear to you?**

💬 **Have you ever been the one to support a friend when things hit rock bottom? What did you do to comfort that friend?**

the girl next door

"Teacher, which is the greatest commandment in the Law?" Jesus replied:
'Love the Lord your God with all your heart and with all your soul and with all your mind.'
This is the first and greatest commandment. And the second is like it: 'Love your neighbor
as yourself.' All the Law and the Prophets hang on these two commandments."
Matthew 22:36-40

Carry each other's burdens, and in this way you will fulfill the law of Christ.
Galatians 6:2

Have you ever carried a weight on your back or held something heavy for a long period of time? I travel a lot, and my luggage and guitar become very burdensome when I'm running from one terminal to the next, frantically trying to catch my flight. I long for someone to take my load for even just a short time, or for one of those airport golf-cart shuttles to stop and let me get on! Wouldn't it be nice if someone would bear your burden? No one would ever feel alone if that were the case. And I believe that is what Christ was calling us to when He told us in Matthew 22 to love our neighbors as ourselves.

neigh•bor (n.)—1) Somebody who lives or is located very close by, for example, on the same street or in the same town; 2) A person, place or thing located next to another or very nearby; 3) A fellow human being.[1]

friend (n.)—1) Somebody who has a close personal relationship of mutual affection and trust with another; 2) Somebody who is not an enemy; 3) Somebody who defends or supports a cause, group, or principle.[2]

In our society, even our neighbors are often strangers. But I don't think Jesus was only referring to the neighbor on your street. I think He also meant the neighbor standing in line at the grocery store, the neighbor sitting at the desk next to you in school, the global neighbor who doesn't speak your language or understand your lifestyle but has a beating heart just like you. These are all neighbors—each of them is a potential *friend*. And the task is simple: Laugh with them when they laugh and cry with them when they cry. Bear their burdens, and you will fulfill the law of Christ.

💬 **In your opinion, what's the difference between a neighbor and a friend? Do you think they should be different?**

💬 **What would it take for you to make friends with the "neighbors" in your life? Time? Attention? Kindness? Do you think Jesus is calling you to bear someone else's burdens? What are you going to do about that?**

Let's pray.

God,

stir up in me a deep compassion. Give me Your heart for people. I confess that my heart is selfish and concerned with things that interest me, but I want to cry with my friends and laugh when they laugh. I want to become a friend who carries their burdens. Please mold me and make me (and if You must, break me) so that I might become like You.

So be it.

Notes
1. *Encarta World English Dictionary.* Developed for Microsoft by Bloomsbury Publishing, 1999, s.v. "neighbor."
2. Ibid., s.v. "friend."

ten:
DON'T HATE ME
because i'm beautiful

jeal•ous (adj.)—1) Feeling bitter and unhappy because of another's advantages, possessions or luck; 2) Feeling suspicious about a rival or competitor's influence, especially in regard to a loved one; 3) Possessively watchful of something; 4) Demanding exclusive loyalty or adherence.[1]

Why is this word "jealousy" synonymous with womanhood? And why are we not outraged and insulted—to the point of actually *changing*—when we hear people say that most women are jealous creatures? I would never describe the male gender (as a whole) as jealous. But with women, it just seems to fit. I don't like it, and I hope you don't either, but we fill the bill all too often.

There are two main sources of female jealousy: beauty and guys. These two categories have the power to ruin friendships and spawn dire enemies. It's sad, really. Let's take a look at each of these jealousy breeders.

Let us behave decently, . . . not in dissension and jealousy. Rather,
clothe yourselves with the Lord Jesus Christ.
Romans 13:13-14

For some reason, we girls feel a sense of superiority when we think we're more beautiful than the next girl. We think, *If I am better than you, then I'll finally feel better about myself.* (Where is the logic in that kind of thinking?) We refuse to accept the fact that we all are beautiful in our own way.

If you don't believe me, then I have an experiment for you. The next time you're in a room full of girls and a really attractive girl walks in the room, look around at all the other girls. Watch their eyes scan her up and down like a piece of meat. (And you thought only guys check out girls!) We all know what they're thinking because we're all thinking the same thing! *Do I look better in my jeans than she does? My hair doesn't look like that, does it? That color looks awful on her. What was she thinking when she left the house this morning? I wonder how much she weighs. I will never be that beautiful even with plastic surgery!* And by the end we either feel better or worse about ourselves. It's truly perplexing to me that another woman—simply by the way she looks—can make me feel confident or disappointed in *myself!*

💬 **We all feel a certain way about our bodies, minds and souls. On a scale of 1 to 10, how do you feel about your beauty?**

1	2	3	4	5	6	7	8	9	10
What Was God Thinking?							Wouldn't Change a Thing		

On a scale of 1 to 10, how do you feel about your intellect and nonphysical attributes?

1	2	3	4	5	6	7	8	9	10
What Was God Thinking?								A+ Baby!	

Check It Out! If you want to learn more about the wonderful body, mind and soul God has given you, check out *Shine: Beautiful Inside and Out* (another Soul Sister Series workbook) by big sis Aly Hawkins.

💬 **Okay, this one may be a little tougher. How do you react when you come across a girl whom you feel surpasses you in brains, talent or beauty? Be honest.**

1	2	3	4	5	6	7	8	9	10
I Hate Her for Life							Jealousy, Shmelousy!		

I have a friend who is stunningly gorgeous and amazingly talented. It's just the cards God has dealt her. One day she told me a story about an experience she had in early adolescence, when she was around 15 years old. *I've* been traumatized by it ever since; I can't imagine what it did to *her*.

My friend (let's call her Jenna) used to sing on the worship team at church. At the end of each service, Jenna would stand around waiting to meet new people, but no one ever approached her. No, let me clarify—no *women* ever approached her. She had her pick of any guy she wanted, but all the females acted very strange and aloof around her. She told me that when I came up and introduced myself (which I always do) she was in such shock and surprise she didn't know what to say. (I guess I have that effect on people.)

Okay, here comes the traumatizing part. One day a young girl approached Jenna and asked if they could talk in private. My friend graciously complied and they slipped around the corner. The young woman started to cry and said, "I just want to repent and ask for your forgiveness." My friend was moved and confused all at once, and she asked her why. The young girl replied, "Because I've hated you since the first day I saw you. You're so beautiful, and I'm so jealous that it has turned into hatred."

🗨 **Do you talk about who's prettier than whom? Do you feel a sense of competition? How do you think other girls look at *you* when you walk in the room? Take some time (at least 10 or 15 minutes) to talk to God about these questions in this space or in your own journal.**

THAT BOY IS MINE

Love is as strong as death, its jealousy unyielding as the grave.
Song of Songs 8:6

Guys seem to be a major source of jealousy among women. I find this fiercely ironic, because none of my guy friends finds it attractive when a woman is jealous.

Most women view men as something to be caught or captured—like a fly in a spider web. They want to *own* him. I hope you can see that's not healthy. It's about time we learned the art of being *friends* with boys. In turn we might just learn how to be friends with girls!

While I have a long list of fantastic girlfriends who have taught me innumerable lessons, I don't think I'd be the same person without my boy friends! Not boyfriends . . . I'm talking about boy *friends*—two (very separate) words. But in order to have meaningful guy friendships, you have to make a conscious choice to feed the feelings of *friendship* and not *romance*.

From the moment I meet a guy who I feel is worth getting to know, I think to myself, *How can I be a part of making him a better man?* And how can he take part in making me a better woman? That's much healthier than thinking, *How can I make him my man?* Does that make sense?

I take my role in my male friends' lives very seriously. I consider it my privilege and duty to help make them better for their future wives. I always tell them that one day they'll thank me for this. For example, when we're walking through a doorway I'll say, "Hey! Let me go first!" When we're getting into the car, I'll offer, "You know, it would be really nice if you opened the car door for me." Or if we're at a nice restaurant, "Why don't you wait to start eating your dinner until I am served mine?" God bless 'em, but sometimes they can be pretty dense! They need a whole lot of practice, and I always consider myself someone they can practice on without fear of repercussion if they don't get it right the first (or tenth) time.

Practice being a feminine, graceful lady with your guy friends. And teach them to practice being a gentleman with you. You never know—all that practicing could pay off and you just might find yourself a keeper. But remember, the goal is not to take home the prize, the goal is friendship.

💬 **How do you feel about friendships with guys? Do you think it's a good idea, or does it cross certain boundaries you've established and want to maintain?**

💬 **Have you ever had a totally platonic (friendly) relationship that did not become romantic? What did you learn from it?**

Have you ever tried to be friends with a guy only to find that eventually one of you wanted more than friendship? What did you learn from that experience?

💬 **What do you think you can learn from guys that you could never learn from girls?**

beautiful**savior**

Because of my profession, I am asked to participate in a lot of worship services. I have to be honest: At times they can become monotonous when you worship night after night. So every once in a while God resorts to drastic measures to restore my wonder of Him. Here's a story of one such time—a time when I had to relearn how to *truly* worship.

I had been at a particular church all day long—so long that I was sick of everyone's face. I just wanted some time to myself. Since it was about an hour before the service was due to start, I thought, *Oh good. I can just sneak away and relax for a second.* But, of course, no sooner did that thought enter my brain than a woman came up to me and said, "We are all gathering to pray before the service. Would you like to join us?"

As awful as it sounds, praying was the last thing I wanted to do at that moment; but I was pretty much obliged to participate, so I reluctantly went. During the prayer time, a woman slipped in the back door. She knelt at the back of the room instead of joining the circle, and with her head bowed, she started whispering—softly, but audibly. Her body rocked back and forth. She obviously really meant what she was saying. Intrigued by this woman's passion, I tuned everyone else out and focused on her prayer. I wanted to be a part of her circle! In an almost chantlike prayer she meditated on the phrase "Jesus, You are so beautiful. . . . You are so beautiful." Over and over she said it. My mind raced to this Scripture:

Search high and low, scan skies and land, you'll find nothing and no one quite like God. The holy angels are in awe before him; he looms immense and august over everyone around him. God of the Angel Armies, who is like you, powerful and faithful from every angle? Your vibrant beauty has gotten inside us—you've been so good to us! We're walking on air! All we are and have we owe to God, Holy God of Israel, our King!
Psalm 89:6-8,17-18 *(The Message)*

I don't know why the thought struck me so profoundly. It was so simple. Jesus is *beautiful*! I've said it and sung it more times than I can count, but that day I realized that not only is Jesus beautiful, but He *is* also beauty. He defines what is and isn't beautiful. All these years I've looked at magazine covers and watched MTV and let them define what I think is beautiful. I've stood in front of a mirror and asked myself, *How do I compare to that standard of beauty?* But that night in the prayer room, it hit me like a flash of lightning: I am only beautiful when I look like Jesus. Because *He is beauty!* I started to pray in my own heart, "Lord, *You* are beautiful; beauty does not exist outside of You. Something can never be truly beautiful if it is not of You. And I want to be like You."

💬 **Who would you describe as the most beautiful woman you know (or have seen on TV or in the movies)? What makes her so gorgeous? Do you know anything about her personal life?**

💬 **What do you think God wants your definition of beauty to be?**

righteousjealousy

Do not make for yourselves an idol in the form of anything the Lord your God has forbidden.
For the Lord your God is a consuming fire, a jealous God.
Deuteronomy 4:23

Scripture refers to God as a "jealous" God. But it's not our beauty or possessions that He's jealous of. He wants *us*—all of us.

So take some advice from me: Don't waste your life thinking jealous thoughts over beauty that fades. Don't let it affect your friendships. Life is too short! Don't give your attention to the things the world tells you are attractive. You will stand before God one day and all earthly splendors will disappear—they won't even be a faint memory compared to His glory. Then (at last) we will in one voice proclaim, "Jesus, *You* are beautiful!" Let's pray.

God,
    forgive me for being jealous of other women because of their beauty. I am sorry I've let that get in the way of potential friendships. Please teach me how to recognize true beauty in everyone, and help me not to be so obsessed with my own. You are the only standard I want to judge by, so please give me Your eyes. I want to see what You see when You look at people.
                    So be it.

Note

1. *Encarta World English Dictionary*. Developed for Microsoft by Bloomsbury Publishing, 1999, s.v. "jealous."

eleven:
good things come
to those who wait

Since ancient times no one has heard, no ear has perceived, no eye has seen any
God besides you, who acts on behalf of those who wait for him. You come to the
help of those who gladly do right, who remember your ways.
Isaiah 64:4-5

"Good things come to those who wait." *Yeah, right!* At least that's what I used to think. It, seemed the only people reciting that mantra had already received the things they were waiting for! Give me someone still in the waiting process, and I doubt you'd hear them say that! But wait, maybe that's the key. When you are still waiting for something, you never know how good it's going to be. So you need someone who's already received the anticipated gift to remind you that all the waiting is worth it.

This half of the workbook is all about friendship, but I'm writing this chapter for those of you who don't have any friends. Lord knows I've been there! This chapter is for those of you who have eaten alone at the lunch table, have been picked last for the soccer game or have been taunted and traumatized by your classmates because you don't drink, smoke or have sex, and you take a stand for your convictions. Maybe you—like me when I was your age—just want one good friend to share your standards and relate to what you're going through; one good friend who won't betray you for the next "cooler" girl who comes along. If that's you, I've got a very important piece of advice: Good things come to those who wait. I promise!

💬 **Do you relate to the girl I just described? Or are you the kind of girl who is so popular and has so many friends that you can't keep up with them all?**

Do you think it would be easier to have lots of friends or none at all? Why? (We both know the obvious answer, but really think about the difficulties and joys of each.)

This chapter isn't just for the social outcasts. Even if you're the girl who has been popular since the day she was born, reading this chapter will help you understand how others feel and experience life. Besides, you never know—the girl you ignore at the lunch table might be the best friend you'll ever have.

Can I ask you to do something? Pull out your Bible and read Matthew 25:31-46. It's a story Jesus told that teaches us how important it is to reach out to those to whom no one else will. I'm warning you—it's a little disconcerting. It deeply convicts me each time I read it. But I think you'll see how incredibly important it is.

> **What are some practical ways you can take this passage to heart? Will you commit to see Jesus in everyone? Or will you continue to treat them as if they didn't matter?**

lessons on waiting

I arrived at my mentor's house on a cold night. She lives in a beautiful A-frame farmhouse with a big brown barn attached to the side. The property is lush with tall sycamore trees and thick green grass. Behind the house she has planted a beautiful rose garden—the type of garden perfect for reflection and steamy cups of coffee. Inside the house, hardwood floors glisten in the sunlight, the stairs creak with age and each bathroom has a freestanding tub. I could go on and on, but I won't. The point I'd like to communicate is how much I *love* her house!

I showed up rather depressed on that cold night. I had three different "friends" (well, people I was *trying* to make friends with, not officially friends yet) who had all flaked on me. Each one had something more important pop up and had to cancel. I tried to pretend that I didn't care, but when I hung up the phone I had to fight back the tears.

I walked into my mentor's kitchen, which always smells of something wonderful, and began to unpack my large bag of grievances. "I feel so lonely tonight," I told her, "Like no one even cares I exist." She looked at me—very sympathetically—and asked me why I felt that way. I told her about how my day had gone. She smiled and said, "Let me tell you a story."

"When my husband and I first decided to move into this area, I found the most adorable house, but it wasn't for sale. I couldn't find anything else that remotely compared to its beauty. I loved it so much that we went so far as to knock on the front door and ask the owners if we could put an offer on it. The woman said she'd think about it. I prayed harder than I've ever prayed that God would give me that house. Finally, the woman called us back and said they were not interested in selling. My heart sank. I thought I knew what was perfect for me and I was angry with God for not giving it to me. But then God spoke to me saying, 'I have something *more* perfect for you.' I didn't think it was possible, but shortly after that incident we found this house.

"Kendall, you really wanted the people who flaked on you today to be your friends, didn't you?" I nodded, a few tears dripping down my cheeks. She continued, "God has a friend that He's preparing for you who is perfect for *you*, just as that first house was a wonderful house, but it wasn't perfect for me. I thought it was, but now that I'm in this one I see how God designed it to fit me just right! He used the lure of my desire to get me excited about moving here. So maybe He'll use your disappointment to help make you ready for the perfect friend He'll bring you."

> Have you ever wanted to be friends with someone more than they wanted to be friends with you? Did you pretend you didn't care? Did you cry yourself to sleep at night? Did you paint on a canvas or write a song? Did you punch your punching bag? We all feel rejected at some point or another, but we handle it differently. What's your method?

IN DEEP WATER

"For I know the plans I have for you," declares the Lord, "plans to prosper you and not to harm you, plans to give you hope and a future. Then you will call upon me and come and pray to me, and I will listen to you."
Jeremiah 29:11-12

In this Scripture, God promises us two things: (1) He knows what He's doing, and (2) He will listen when we pray to Him.

God would not take us to the deep end of the swimming pool only to let us drown. If the water's deep, then maybe He wants to teach us to swim! Sometimes we grow too comfortable in the shallow end. We have our little floaties on our arms and our feet can touch the bottom without our head going under. Those are the times in life when we have abundant friends, plenty of money and everything's going our way.

For some reason (okay, for a lot of reasons), God doesn't like to leave us there very long. He starts moving down toward the deep end, shouting, "Come on! Follow me!" Our anxiety starts to rise, because there's no telling what might happen in the deep waters. But He gets us down there—and guess what happens? We never want to go back to the kiddie pool again! We dread the unknown until we accept it, and then we end up loving what He gives us.

When I look back on all the friendless years I endured, all the lonely days and nights, I am extremely grateful for them. God taught me more about myself in those times than I could have learned otherwise. When friends are plentiful and our schedules are packed with activities, we don't examine our souls and we don't cry out to God in desperation.

💬 **Can you even imagine a day when you will thank God for your loneliness? What would it take to get you to that point? What lessons have you learned so far?**

don't forget to
say please

Do not be anxious about anything, but in everything, by prayer and petition, with thanksgiving, present your requests to God. And the peace of God, which transcends all understanding, will guard your hearts and your minds in Christ Jesus.
Philippians 4:6

Remember the second thing we learned from Jeremiah 29:11-12? God promises to listen when we pray to Him. Have you ever prayed for a friend? Chances are you've spent a lot of time whining to God (and probably everyone else) that you're in need. But have you ever actually *prayed* about this need?

💬 Write a prayer to God, asking Him for a friend. Tell Him everything you hope for. Tell Him about your loneliness. Tell Him what it's like to go to school every day and come home without a really great friend to share it all with. Pour your heart out to Him—He has promised He will listen.

I remember being in youth group and the youth pastor led me in a similar prayer. A few months later, a new family started attending our church and they had a daughter just my age. At first it was awkward because neither of us knew how to be friends, but in retrospect that was the perfect plan of God. He brought us together so that we could learn from each other.

Don't become frustrated if it doesn't seem God answers your prayer right away. Remember, God's timing is best! He may know that you need to spend a little longer in the deep end with Him before you're ready for what He has planned for you. Be patient—good things come to those who wait!

the missing piece

One of my favorite children's books of all time is Shel Silverstein's *The Missing Piece Meets the Big O*. The story begins with a triangle who believes she is somebody's missing piece. Her deepest desire is to roll with someone, because she thinks she cannot roll alone. A lot of funny Pac-Man-looking characters come along, but she just doesn't seem to fit with any of them. Then one day she meets the Big O, who doesn't want or need anything from her. So the Big O gives her some advice: "Try learning to roll on your own!"

The missing piece protests that she's not shaped for rolling—she has sharp corners! But the Big O tells her, "Shapes have a way of changing and corners have a way of wearing off." Then he leaves her and she's all alone again. I guess that was just the last straw for the missing piece, because all of a sudden she decides to take the Big O's advice to heart. Slowly but surely, she learns to roll on her own, and then she joins the Big O—but not as a missing piece anymore!

How might this story apply to your own life? Do you ever feel like that missing piece, just waiting for a friend who will give your life meaning?

We simply cannot be somebody else's missing piece. No friendship will be successful when it is need driven. If you need another person to feel complete, then you will constantly be disappointed. Be your own person, develop your own interests and talents, and I bet you'll find a friend.

Does anything pique your interests? Drawing, snowboarding, riding horses, playing guitar, shopping, cooking, eating, fencing, learning karate, talking on the phone, watching movies, candlemaking, snail racing—anything? No matter what you're passionate about, I guarantee you'll find someone else in the world who shares a similar interest! Then you will have found a friend. Friends can't just sit and stare at each other—they need to *do* things together. Maybe that is a part of the lesson God wants to teach you.

God gives each of us wonderful gifts and expects us to use them to the fullest potential. And once you find a passion for something—your expertise—you won't care if you sit alone at the lunch table. You might not have friends everywhere you go, but you will feel confident knowing that you have friends with whom you share something very special.

Let's pray.

God,
   I am so grateful for all the blessings You've given me. You really know just what I need right when I need it, so I place my desires at the foot of Your Cross. Please help me to leave them there. Help me see You in every person I meet, and teach me to treat each of them as I'd treat You.
                              So be it.

twelve: the art of being honest and available

You adulterous people, don't you know that friendship with the world is hatred toward God? Anyone who chooses to be a friend of the world becomes an enemy of God.

James 4:4

Ouch! That is some strong language; I think we'd better pay attention. It doesn't sound like God's kidding around. It's time we look at what characteristics God is looking for in a friend.

💬 **What do you think James meant by "friendship with the world?" Do you care more about yourself and your own life than you care about the things of God?**

💬 **If God asked you to give up something, would you do it for Him? What if your best gal pal asked something of you—would you deny her? Do you think it's easier to say no to God or to a friend? Why?**

open on aisle five

I have one friend who is always available whenever I need her. It is the most comforting thought to know that I can call her morning, noon or night and she'll pick up and be ready to talk. Friends need to be available for each other. If you don't have time for your friends, then I'm betting they won't stay your friends very long.

If you want to work on becoming a better friend, start by paying attention to your friends' needs. When a friend calls, don't turn your phone to silent. If you're not in the mood to talk about her problems *again*, that's okay—just remember all the times when she was sick of talking to you but answered anyway!

There's a story in the Old Testament about a guy who knew how to be available—and we're not talking about being willing to talk on the phone—this guy was available for God Himself! Pull out your Bible and read this story for yourself—you'll find it in 1 Samuel 3. Go on—I'll wait.

Talk about the "phone call" of your life! That would be better than Ed McMahon showing up on your doorstep with a check for one million dollars! God knew Samuel's heart, and He wasn't frustrated that it took him three times to get it right. (Sam would have probably kept waking the old man if Eli hadn't clued him in.)

One of the greatest gifts you can give a friend is just to be there in times of trial. You don't have to know the right thing to say and you don't have to make everything better, but a good friend gives of her time. Ironically, that's what God wants from us too—our availability. He just wants to be with us.

💬 **Are you available for your friends? If someone called you up in the middle of the night, how would you respond?**

    A. "Sorry—closed for business!"
    B. "Call back in the morning . . . when I'm awake."
    C. "What's up?"

💬 **When God calls, how do you typically respond? Like Samuel, do you say, "Speak, for your servant is listening"?**

Save me, O Lord, from lying lips and deceitful tongues.
Psalm 120:2

Another extremely important—often undervalued—quality in a friend is honesty. Honesty is the ability to say what no one else would dare to say, not out of spite or rudeness, but out of *love*. Let me tell you, when you find a friend who will speak the truth, you'd better hold on to *her* for dear life. The truth does hurt, but that's no reason to stop listening to it.

Let's go back to our story about Samuel to see how much God values honesty. Read 1 Samuel 3:11-18.

💬 **Have you ever had to be painfully honest with a friend? How did she respond? What did you learn from the experience?**

Samuel spoke the truth—even though he was scared to tell Eli because he cared about him. C. S. Lewis says in *The Screwtape Letters*, "The act of cowardice is all that matters; the emotion of fear is, in itself, no sin."[1] In other words, being afraid to say what you have to say is okay. But if you let that fear rule you and decide not to open your mouth, that's not okay.

Of course, we should always use tact and good timing. You shouldn't just blurt things out, but commit inside your heart to always graciously speak the truth, no matter how painful. That is being a true friend. If a friend gets mad at you for that, there's nothing you can do but pray that God softens her heart and that He teaches her through it.

the art of friendship

This is a story I wrote for one of my best friends. It's written as a simple children's parable. I tend to learn best from children's books. (While all the really "mature Christians" are reading 2,000-page seventeenth-century theological books, you can find me in the kiddie section at Barnes & Noble, sitting at a pint-size picnic table, probably sniffling because the little boy's love made the stuffed rabbit real.) Anyway, I hope you enjoy . . .

Leonard the Lion and Danny the Dog
A tale of friendship by Kendall Payne

There once was a powerful lion, Leo was his name—
Leonard to be exact, but he liked being called Leo just the same.
Now his best friend's name was Danny; "Dan the Dog" some would say.
You could call him Dan, Danny or Daniel; I doubt he would complain.

They both had tails and fur and paws, and loved to run real fast;
They both were sure, the day they met, their friendship was going to last.
Now Leo was King of the Jungle, and Danny was the top dog at the farm;
But they were different (you'll soon see), which caused them some alarm.

Leo was strong and made all the rules (which everyone always obeyed);
Dan was kind and caring instead; he made sure there was plenty of play.
Leonard would growl if anyone dared to step even a hair out of line;
Danny would smile if anyone failed—"Maybe you'll get it next time!"

And so life went on for the lion and dog; both were quite happy I'd say.
They liked how they lived, and they liked how they ruled,
Until one quite unfortunate day . . .

The chickens stopped laying eggs; the cats didn't want to catch mice;
The rooster slept through his alarm 'cause he was up too late last night.
Then the cows stopped giving milk, and all the pigs went on a diet;
Danny's whole farm was falling apart—the animals wanted to riot!
He tried being nice, he tried being sweet, but they wouldn't listen to him!
Dan knew he was going to need help fast, so he ran to Leo, his friend.

"Leo, please! Tell me your secret—you don't know what the farm is like!
The chickens and cats and cows and pigs have all up and gone on strike!
I think I've been *too* nice, a little *too* sweet—now no one does what I say;
They only laugh when I'm being stern or when they have misbehaved."
"Oh, Danny boy," said Leo the King, "So you want to even the score?
I'd be happy to teach you all that you need, but first you must hear me

ROARRRRRRR!"

Leo was strong and Leo was firm, but this Lion was also quite smart.
"I rule with my roar as all lions do, but *you* need to find your own bark!"
"My own bark?" said Dan sheepishly, "I guess I've just never thought
That I was anything that special . . . so I never practiced a whole lot!"
"Now's as good a time as any," the big lion said with a grin;
And he drove that message loud and clear until Danny finally did learn.
Sure enough, when Dan went home, he went home a different dog;
Everyone noticed immediately and got back to doing their jobs.

And so life went on for the lion and dog; both were quite happy I'd say.
They liked how they lived, and they liked how they ruled,
Until one quite unfortunate day . . .

This time Leonard needed a friend to show him a thing or two;
Danny arrived just in time, as Leonard cried out, "BoooooHooooo!"
He asked, "What ever is the matter?" as Leo wiped tears from his eyes.
"Nobody wants to play with me—they're all too scared they'll die!
I chew 'em out and I spit 'em up, or have I got it upside down?
Anyway, they all have said that I'm not much fun to be around.
'But I'm a lion,' I tell them, 'And lions are ferocious beasts!'
I guess that's just the way I am, and that's how I'll always be."

Danny looked at Leo's sad face (all alone there in his cave),
Then the thought hit him hard— "Leo, I can teach you to play!"
The lion's eyes beamed bright with hope; he gave an excited roar.
He smiled as big as a lion can smile and said, "What are we waiting for?"
First Danny took him to the river's edge, and made Leo show his teeth.
The water reflected Leo's frightening smile—and he saw what others see.
Then Danny filed Leo's long nails until they weren't so scary and sharp.
(Leo wasn't sure about this at first, but he trusted Danny's heart.)

Then Danny took Leo to a field for their first friendly wrestling match;
When Leo pounced upon Danny, he laughed and ignored the scratch.
He said, "Playing is not about winning; It's only about having fun."
Leonard realized the truth in his words and felt very, very dumb.
From that day on, Leo never bit or scratched or ate his friends.
And thanks to Danny's instructions, He was never left out again.

And so life went on for the lion and dog; both were quite happy I'd say;
They liked how they lived, and they liked how they ruled—
Best of friends for the rest of their days.
The moral of this story, if you'd like to know:
If you find a friend who's different from you,
In time, your similarities will show.

Well our time has come to an end! Thank you so much for joining me on this journey. I know I've had fun sharing my stories and insights learned through trial and error. I hope you've learned a little and laughed a lot along the way, and may you continue to do so always!

Let me pray for you now.

Can you think of a little story like this about you and your best friend? Think about each of your best traits and how you balance each other out. Your story doesn't have to rhyme—just try it! If nothing else, you'll both get a laugh out of it. Write it out on another piece of paper or in your journal.

God,
   I ask with all of my heart that You would give this young woman wisdom beyond her years—not wisdom of this world, but wisdom from You. Help her to follow You in a world that doesn't always encourage that. Grow her into a mature Christian woman, confident in Your ways and truth. Even with all of our humanness and all of our failings and frailty, we really love You, Lord. So be it.

Note

1. C. S. Lewis, *The Screwtape Letters* (San Francisco, CA: HarperSanFrancisco, 2001), p 163.

Soul Sister Leader Tips

"Their leader will be one of their own; their ruler will arise from among them. I will bring him near and he will come close to me, for who is he who will devote himself to be close to me?" declares the Lord.
Jeremiah 30:21

Whether this is your first time leading a group or you're a seasoned veteran, we're glad you've decided to embrace the challenge. You may be a mom, mentor or even a young woman yourself, but if God has called you to invest time, energy and emotion into the lives of young women, He will make your sacrifice well worth it!

The Soul Sister series can be done alone, with a big sis (mentor), your mom or one or more friends. If you are leading a group through these workbooks, your primary roles will be to organize a meeting time and to facilitate how you spend that time. We've put together a few tips to assist you in the process.

Suggestions for Group Study

1. Do your best to make the environment conducive to talking about the areas in the girls' lives that hinder them from growing spiritually and from finding their identity. Stress the importance of confidentiality—what is shared stays within the group.

2. Before each meeting, read through the session and mark questions and sections that you think particularly apply to your group. During the meeting, don't spend too much time on one section unless it is obvious that God is working in people's lives at a particular moment. We all lead very busy lives; respect the girls in your group by beginning and ending meetings on time.

3. Make time for fun! If you find that your group gets antsy easily, utilize the bulk of the time on activities, creative exercises and fellowship. Remember that relationships will be the most important thing these girls will take away from your group time.

4. You can't stress enough the importance of writing in a journal! This simple exercise will help the girls process their thoughts, apply what they're learning and leave a record of how far they've come.

5. Always begin and end the meetings with prayer. If your group is small, have the whole group pray together. If it is larger than 10 members, form groups of 2 to 4 to share and pray for one another.

6. Be prepared. Pray for your preparation and for the girls in your group during the week.

7. Don't let one person dominate the discussion. Ask God to help you draw out the quiet ones without putting them on the spot.

8. Spend time each meeting worshiping God, either at the beginning or end of the meeting. Don't be nervous! If you feel uncomfortable leading the group with an instrument, utilize worship CDs or invite one or more girls to lead everyone in worship.

Suggestions for Mentoring Relationships

As stated earlier, this workbook lends itself for use in mentoring relationships. Women in particular are admonished in Scripture to train younger women (see Titus 2:3-5).

• A mentoring relationship could be arranged through a system set up by a church or youth ministry.

• If you'd like to mentor a younger woman or be mentored by someone who exemplifies the Christlike life, don't be shy! Mentoring doesn't have to be a formal process. Take the initiative and ask if you can meet every so often to go through this workbook together. More often than not, the relationship you build will far outlast the pages contained in this book.

• Don't shy away from mentoring simply because your walk with the Lord is less than perfect. We're all in process! God has commanded us to disciple new and growing believers, and He doesn't stipulate how "mature" we must be first. Don't worry— Matthew 28:20 says that God promises to be with you through thick and thin.

• Once you agree to mentor a young woman, be prepared to learn as much or more than she does! You will both be blessed by the mentoring relationship built on the relationship you have together in the Lord.